THE

MW01132264

Civil Leadership in Action

Tiana Sanchez with:

Deborah K. Ford, PhD - Andy Fee
Natalie Parks, PhD, BCBA-D, LP - Dr. Nicole Yeldell Butts
Paula Valle Castañon - Mark Maes - and Marina St Cyr

ATG

PUBLISHING

The New C-Suite : Civil Leadership in Action

Copyright © 2024 by Tiana Sanchez.

For information contact :
ATG Publishing - info@atgpublishing.com - http://www.atgpublishing.com

ISBN: 9781991123060

First Edition: September 2024

10 9 8 7 6 5 4 3 2 1

Contents

Introduction

The New C-Suite is Addressing a Challenge

Traditional business paradigms: Short-term gains instead of long-term success

Traditional business paradigms have increasingly prioritized short-term gains, emphasizing profit maximization above all else. Consequently, there has been a notable neglect of long-term considerations and essential human elements in the workplace, including culture, ethics, and social responsibility. Furthermore, traditional models often fail to address emerging diversity challenges, viewing them merely as costs rather than valuable investments. In today's landscape, there is a pressing need for robust, long-term sustainability practices to ensure enduring success.

Let's take a renowned case study in traditional business

practices: General Electric at the time of being led by "Neutron Jack" Welch. Welch introduced an approach known as 'shareholder capitalism,' which prioritized satisfying stockholders and significantly increasing GE's share value. This approach views labor as a cost to be minimized for greater profit. However, perpetual cost-cutting harms morale and drives talent away, ultimately shrinking the organization and reversing the short-term gains.

Like General Electric, Boeing embraced shareholder capitalism for growth. Despite initial success, they faced long-term quality problems which led to a reputation for poor-quality planes, crashes, and loss of life. Even Boeing employees acknowledge their lack of confidence in the products manufactured during this period.

These are well-documented examples of the long-term costs of traditional practices. Yet, numerous organizations still employ them, notably through top-down leadership. However, much like traditional business practices, these leadership styles often neglect crucial factors affecting long-term organizational sustainability.

Going Deeper and Moving Beyond Traditional Leadership

These critical factors, often dubbed "the Intangibles," are less visible than traditional business metrics. Tangibles like revenue and profit are straightforward, while intangibles such as culture and leadership exert significant but less observable influence. Recent research underscores this, indicating that leaders often prioritize tangible day-to-day operations, neglecting opportunities to foster intangible elements like coaching and shared vision.

Despite consistent research advocating for change, why do we hesitate to embrace it? Change is inherently difficult; it's simpler to stick with what's familiar until it fails, leaving us no choice but to adapt. Having a structured framework eases the transition.

Civil Leadership

The Civil Leadership Model is a comprehensive framework that integrates intangible elements into the business model. This framework is made up of three pillars and it empowers leaders to leverage the benefits of intangibles, exemplify productive behaviors, and integrate established best practices. Additionally, it proactively addresses evolving societal demands, ensuring the organization remains responsive and adaptable.

Pillar 1: Your Approach to Leadership

When we adopt a community-first leadership approach, we focus on the benefits of serving others. An example of this approach is the Servant Leadership model. Servant Leadership is a modern leadership model emphasizing serving the organization or employees over profits. It adopts a bottom-up approach, where leaders serve their teams rather than vice versa, earning authority through trust rather than hierarchical power. This fosters collaboration, coaching, and innovation, empowering employees and prioritizing well-being. Servant Leaders cultivate future leaders through traits like empathy, listening, stewardship, and commitment to personal growth.

In this approach, leaders garner respect, foster a shared vision, and build trust with their team. Incorporating employee input into the decision-making processes results in better outcomes. Employees feel appreciated and valued, and an environment promoting individual growth is created.

Organizations such as Hershey, Coca-Cola, Starbucks, Nordstrom, and Marriott International have embraced Servant Leadership to enhance their culture, sustainability, and profitability.

What does a servant leader look like?

- A person of character embodies the principles of servant leadership by prioritizing integrity, ethics, and humility, while serving a higher purpose within the organization.
- They put people first, demonstrating care and support for employees' growth and goals.
- They have effective communication skills. These skills are essential for a servant leader to listen, speak, and solicit feedback from their team.

- They are a compassionate collaborator. A servant leader fosters relationships, supports diversity and inclusion, and navigates workplace conflicts.
- They use foresight, anticipating future challenges and maintaining a clear organizational vision, ready to take decisive action when necessary.
- They are a systems thinker who thrives in complex environments and employs strategic thinking to lead organizational change effectively.
- They lead with moral authority, a servant leader builds trust by setting high standards, delegating responsibility, and fostering a culture of accountability within the workforce.

Pillar 2: Being Socially Responsible

Organizations adopt social responsibility goals (or ESG goals) to improve the world around them while achieving business success. Think of the likes of Salesforce, Target, and Ben & Jerry. They show us that it is possible to do both! In doing so, they have been able to enhance their sustainability practices whilst improving community welfare in the wider world. At the same time, their traditional business metrics (e.g. revenue and profit) are still strong.

We still have more to do. A 2023 study found that there is much room for improvement in this area. Only 16% of US organizations prioritize social responsibility, compared to over 50% in Germany,

France, Belgium, and Canada.

Keep in mind that social responsibility is increasingly vital for younger generations of employees and leaders. Socially responsible organizations find it easier to attract top talent and cultivate goodwill with the public and potential customers. Additionally, social responsibility can be a key factor in attracting new investors.

How can an organization be more socially responsible?

- Implement a business code of ethics to guide employee conduct on issues such as ethics, values, environment, diversity, employee respect, and customer service.
- Demonstrating commitment to environmental protection involves developing policies and practices, potentially supported by comprehensive sustainability reports.
- Engage suppliers to adhere to responsible behavior standards (such as fair pricing).
- Strategically allocate donations to causes aligned with business values.
- Ensure that marketing efforts uphold fairness, honesty, and company integrity.
- Ensure that actions align with communications.

Pillar 3: Harnessing Diversity and Creative Synthesis

Creative synthesis, in this body of work, is when you combine different ideas, differing perspectives, elements, or pieces of information to create something new and original. This process involves taking bits and pieces from different sources and mixing them in a new way to create something unique. It embraces diversity, creativity, and uniqueness. Organizations which embrace diversity have found various benefits that are reflected in their traditional business metrics:

- Organizations with diverse boards experience 53% higher returns on equity and 14% higher earnings.
- Companies with women on their boards demonstrate better average growth rates.
- US and Canadian companies with ethnically diverse executive teams have a 20% higher chance of achieving earnings above the national median.
- Ethnically and racially diverse teams outperform industry norms by 35%.

These outcomes are largely attributed to enhanced decision-making abilities.

While homogenous groups may make decisions more quickly and confidently, diverse groups, despite taking longer and engaging in debates, ultimately arrive at better decisions by considering a broader range of perspectives and alternatives.

Diversity includes tangible aspects such as age, ethnicity, and gender, as well as intangible elements like perspectives, experiences, and approaches. Ensuring that both tangible and intangible advantages are being harnessed allows an organization to see greater returns from the diversity advantage.

How can an organization best embrace diversity?

- Be open-minded. Recognize and challenge your biases. Welcome new ideas and perspectives.
- Acknowledge the role of diversity in fostering innovation and creativity. Show that everyone's contributions are valued.
- Maintain curiosity about the unknown.
- Practice inclusiveness: Invite everyone to the table when making impactful decisions, even those who traditionally wouldn't have input.
- Show empathy and active listening. Understand the needs and experiences of others.
- Volunteer to assist others, promoting connection with team members and the broader community.
- Advocate for diversity and inclusion, both internally and externally.
- Empower others to act.

Combining the Pillars: Is it Possible?

Adopting the above practices might seem daunting. Transitioning to a new organizational style will require effective change management strategies. Nevertheless, it is possible to make this change and support effective practices within your organization.

Numerous organizations have successfully embraced this change and paved the road for others. They have done so by earning a certification as a "B Corp" (Beneficial Corporation) organization.

What is a "B Corp" Organization?

These are businesses committed to enhancing society through positive social and environmental impacts. The certification process, initiated in 2006, has seen over 8,000 companies worldwide gain certification. This designation involves a thorough assessment of the organization's social and environmental performance, public transparency, and legal accountability. To maintain certification, companies must adapt to evolving environmental and social standards, as the requirements are updated periodically.

Research indicates that B Corps demonstrate strong financial performance, often on par with or even surpassing traditional businesses. They are more likely to experience growth in both their workforce and revenue, outperforming conventional businesses in terms of job creation and sales. B Corps exhibit greater resilience to disruptions, with over 95% remaining in business in 2023 compared to 88% of non-B Corps. Their emphasis on people and social impact positions B Corps for long-term sustainability, viewing these factors as valuable assets for enduring success.

B Corp Case Study- Unique leverage in the food industry

Danone, a renowned B Corp yogurt company, is a French multinational with a workforce exceeding 100,000 employees worldwide. Leveraging this status, Danone successfully negotiated reduced interest rates on their US$ 2 billion financing in 2018, based on verified improvements in their global environmental and social impact. Additionally, creditors agreed to further reduce interest rates for subsidiaries that attained B Corp certification.

Connecting the Dots

Whether you choose to explore B-Corp certification or explore the three pillars or agree with this view on civil leadership, you will never look at leadership the same way – that is my hope. This collection of chapters represents the unique perspectives, expertise, and experiences of each author.

Starting with Visionary Leadership, you'll explore leadership theories with a new lens that addresses the challenges of our data-driven, fast-paced, globally diverse environment.

Civil Leadership is at the core of aligning community, social responsibility, and individual creativity, connecting business principles with global initiatives for longevity and sustainability.

Inclusive Leadership invites you to gaze upon this critical leadership practice with fresh eyes and focus on the importance and creation of an inclusive organizational culture, through the encouragement, enablement, and valuing of employee ideas.

Ethical Leadership explores the vital importance of ethics in modern business, the link between ethical leadership and innovation, and guidance for building and maintaining a thriving culture of integrity.

Socially Responsible Leadership delves into the seven behaviors of socially responsible leaders, a critical component of the modern C-Suite.

Impactful Leadership describes a leader who doesn't lead through hierarchical power, but through earning their teams' trust by showing up with care and support.

Holistic Leadership dares us to integrate the key fundamentals of business—what they are, how they work, and why they are essential to success in business, family, life, legacy, and purpose.

Change Leadership focuses on workplace changes that are required to move people in a new direction that ultimately require perspective adjustments in order to advance forward.

This literary work is designed for leaders across all levels, industries, and countries. Whether you're a pragmatic leader, a pacesetter, or a visionary, this book speaks directly to you. It's crafted for the Head Coach, the Dean, the Non-Profit Leader, the Startup CEO, the Franchise Owner, and even the head of a political party.

This is a serious book with a personal touch, where each author brings a unique perspective on civil leadership in their own distinct way. While the authors share similar ideals, their vastly different experiences make for a rich and varied read. You'll laugh, you'll be challenged, and you'll find yourself eager to turn the page.

It's a book meant to be read together with others, inviting discussion and reflection. And the best part? You don't have to read it in order—jump in wherever you feel inspired!

Visionary Leadership

By Deborah K. Ford, PhD

Leadership is the art of influence, the power to inspire and guide others toward a common goal. It involves not only navigating change, setting a clear direction, aligning people with organizational objectives, and solving problems, but also inspiring grit, and pivoting to the new while driving collective success.

While management deals with the intricacies of complexity, planning, organizing, and staffing to ensure smooth operations, true leadership transcends these functions, steering the organization through unrelenting transformation to meet the demands of continuous innovation.

In the 90s and early 2000s, organizations recognized the crucial need to nurture exceptional leaders. These organizations invested heavily in identifying and developing leadership talent exclusively within the upper echelon of employees. Assessment centers became central to this effort, offering rigorous evaluations through structured exercises and real-world simulations. This inward focus emphasized traits and behaviors that could motivate teams and grab recognition from higher ups.

This outdated approach fails to keep pace with industry advancements and the growing demand for leadership behaviors and talent. The retirement of baby boomers, born between 1946 and 1964, is creating a significant leadership vacuum. By 2030, all baby boomers will reach the traditional retirement age of 65, according to the U.S. Census Bureau. A TaxTalent study revealed that 35% of the tax workforce comprises baby boomers, with 69% of those aged 58 or older likely to retire within four years. Fry (2020) reported that 28.6 million baby boomers were retired in the third quarter of 2020, with an annual growth of two million, increasing the demand for proficient leaders.

In addition to this, gone are the days when employees stay with a single organization, climbing the corporate ladder with over a decade of experience. The departure of baby boomer leaders presents a critical challenge for organizations to develop millennial and Gen Z talent. Identifying high-potential leaders within a competitive and shrinking talent pool and maturing that talent for executive roles often occurs over a drastically reduced timeline. The lengthy time to develop leaders contributes to leadership skill gaps.

The demands for leadership require promoting empowerment at all levels to meet the rapid pace of change and innovation.

Leadership is dynamic and evolving, crucial to the success and growth of any organization. It must shift from a narrow focus on personal attributes and individual advancement to a broader, more altruistic perspective. This change is reflected in literature on civil leadership, organizational culture and diversity, equity, and inclusion. Effective leaders today must elevate others, support teams beyond their direct control, and remove barriers to collective success. This shift underscores the importance of leaders who prioritize team value, exhibit humility and empathy, and foster trust in all aspects of leadership.

Further, contemporary leadership must emphasize engagement with diffused and diverse stakeholders, addressing immense complexities driven by technological advancements. The digital age has revolutionized leadership practices, necessitating skills like adaptability, technological proficiency, and the ability to build cohesive and productive geographically dispersed teams.

Undeniably, today's workforces are often geographically dispersed with multi-national representation. Geographically dispersed teams frequently produce cost savings, access to global talent pools, and the rise of remote work facilitated by technology. Even colocated teams include globally sourced talent servicing a diverse marketplace.

With all this in mind, this chapter presents leadership theories with a new lens that addresses the challenges of our data-driven, fast-paced, globally diverse environment. In my executive coaching efforts, I have applied insights from the GLOBE project, initiated by Robert House in the early 1990s, to focus on both universally valued and culturally specific leadership behaviors and attributes. These include Charismatic/Value-Based Leadership, Team-Oriented Leadership, and Participative Leadership. The GLOBE study, encompassing data from over 17,000 leaders in 951 organizations across 62 countries, highlights essential traits for effective leadership worldwide.

In my leadership work, I have built on the foundational GLOBE study, reshaping its concepts to prepare leaders for business impact. I aim to reexamine these attributes through a modern lens, focusing on qualities needed to navigate today's complex environment:

- Leading Disruptions Without Being Disruptive:
  - Thriving amidst uncertainty and ambiguity, not just surviving.
- Building Trust: The Foundation of Influence and Effectiveness:
  - Emphasizing integrity, honesty, ethical behavior, and empathy.
- Cultivating a Culture of Visionary Thinking:
  - Inspiring and aligning a team around a compelling

future vision, while executing visionary thinking requires translating that vision into actionable steps with precision, skill, and collaborative effort.

Through this exploration, we uncovered the essential leadership qualities required to excel in today's complex, rapidly changing, and globally interconnected world. This sets the stage for leaders who transform vision into reality and inspire their teams to achieve extraordinary outcomes.

Leading Disruptions without being Disruptive

In our fast-paced, tech-driven world, businesses face tough competition on a global scale. Harvard Business (2024) reports that 68% of leaders must not only endure but embrace ambiguity and uncertainty. The capability to define and operationalize ambiguity is paramount, accelerating time to productivity and fostering a resilient organization.

Additionally, the introduction and advances in machine learning and AI present even more disruption, complexity, and uncertainty for leaders. In fact, data from Microsoft and LinkedIn's 2024 Work Trend Index reveals that 75% of knowledge workers now use AI in their roles, with a staggering 46% having adopted it within the past six months. This rapid adoption of AI in the workplace highlights the transformative impact of this technology on the modern workforce.

Adaptive leadership promotes resilience and flexibility, helping organizations not only survive but thrive amid rapid change. Adaptive leaders excel at diagnosing situations, recognizing patterns, and adjusting their strategies accordingly. Research shows that such leaders are adept at mobilizing others to tackle tough challenges, encouraging experimentation, and learning from failures (Heifetz, Grashow, & Linsky, 2009). The adaptive leadership framework emphasizes five key concepts essential for navigating challenging environments:

Diagnosing the System: Understanding the complexities of the organizational environment.

Regulating Distress: Keeping stress levels productive to encourage growth without overwhelming team members.

Maintaining Disciplined Attention: Ensuring focus on critical issues without getting distracted.

Giving the Work Back to the People: Empowering team members to take ownership of their work and decisions.

Protecting Voices of Leadership from Below: Encouraging input and feedback from all organizational levels, fostering a culture of inclusivity and diverse perspectives.

In my consulting work, I helped an international telecommunications client facing high turnover, slow hiring, and declining employee sentiment. Our analysis led us to shift from simple training to creating appealing "digital and agile" job titles and redefining team workflows. The results were remarkably positive, akin to a collective sigh of relief from the workforce.

Leaders who embrace uncertainty, challenge the status quo, and foster collaboration and diversity are best positioned to drive innovation and success in today's dynamic environment. By understanding and applying adaptive leadership principles, leaders can navigate the complexities of modern organizations, inspire their teams, and turn visionary ideas into impactful realities.

Diagnosing the System

The true test of leadership is navigating intense competition. Visionary leaders must master their industry and harness change to drive their organizations forward. This requires humility and stakeholder engagement, seeking insights from employees, customers, suppliers, and other stakeholders to foster trust and cooperation.

Strong dynamic capabilities for sensing and seizing opportunities equip organizations to navigate turbulence and maintain a competitive advantage. For ages, skilled leaders have analyzed their organization's core strengths and vulnerabilities, using tools like SWOT (Strengths, Weaknesses, Opportunities, Threats) analysis to chart the path forward. Additionally, the PESTLE (Political, Economic, Social, Technological, Legal, Environmental) framework is a rigorous methodology for environmental scanning.

In my executive coaching, I've found that developing habits for active listening and scanning can be incredibly impactful. With a Citigroup executive, we scheduled monthly deep analysis sessions, included relevant podcasts and journals in her weekly routine, and provided skills for listening and probing stakeholders. These habits helped ensure she stays current with relevant insights and industry trends. Plus, the habits became more second nature. You will often find that focusing on a couple of behavioral changes as habits can be more lasting, which enhances reliability.

Regulating Distress

As an organizational psychologist that also works in HR, I have a bird's eye view of the organizational dynamics, the triggers, and the strains and stressors that emerge across the workforce. In my observations, stress will present itself invariably over time and can either build resilience or shatter resolve. Masterful leaders will address distress and redirect the team towards greatness. Consider the visionary leaders of Silicon Valley, whose companies are at the edge of innovation. They understand challenges are inevitable, and that a certain degree of productive stress is necessary to sharpen focus and ignite creativity. Yet, the truly talented and prolific leaders also recognize there's a delicate balance between pushing their teams and pushing them too far. They're careful to inspire without overwhelming.

Impactful leaders possess the unique ability to transform challenges into a driving force for success. They set ambitious yet achievable goals, providing the resources and support necessary for success. They offer consistent feedback, not as a tool of criticism, but as a compass guiding their teams towards ever-greater heights.

Effective leaders play a pivotal role in fostering team self-efficacy and confidence while mitigating doubt and stress. Through verbal persuasion, leaders can express faith in the team's capabilities, provide encouragement, and frame challenges as opportunities for growth. Leaders are able to regulate team stress by promoting an open communication climate, acknowledging concerns, reframing stressors as challenges within the team's capabilities, and providing instrumental support (Breevaart & Bakker, 2018; Edmondson, 1999). Ultimately, leaders who cultivate a mastery-oriented team climate, facilitate shared positive emotions and proactively address self-doubt to enhance confidence and resilience (Salanova et al., 2011; Tasa et al., 2007).

At Google, leaders foster an environment where "psychological safety" is paramount, encouraging open dialogue and creating a space where team members can voice concerns without fear of judgment. This simple act of vulnerability disarms the corrosive effects of unchecked stress, allowing teams to confront obstacles head-on, united in their pursuit of solutions.

Similarly, organizations can implement programs and wellness initiatives that restore energy and creativity. During my time at Adobe, I developed immense pride in their commitment to employee well-being and work-life balance. The company offers flexible work arrangements, including remote work options, which 75% of employees value enough to consider relocating for. Adobe's comprehensive approach includes generous time-off policies and wellness programs like "Wellness Reimbursement" for fitness activities.

Mental health support is a key pillar of Adobe's wellbeing strategy, with resources such as employee assistance programs (EAP) and access to wellbeing apps. Adobe fosters a culture of taking breaks, exemplified by initiatives like "Global Wellbeing Week" and company-wide days off. Innovative office spaces feature relaxation areas like "Somodome pods" for restorative breaks. These efforts contribute to Adobe's high employee engagement score of 86%, surpassing the technology sector average of 74%. Additionally, Adobe's low employee turnover rate of 10% compared to the industry average of 13% further demonstrates the effectiveness of its work-life balance initiatives.

If done well, stress drives growth and reveals the true capabilities of teams. The path to greatness is riddled with challenges. Those who embrace those challenges as opportunities to cultivate resilience, innovation, and a deep sense of purpose will grow stronger from the experiences. It is not the absence of stress that defines greatness, but the ability to harness its power, to transform distress into drive, and to emerge from adversity with strength, greater clarity, and sharpened knowledge.

Maintaining Disciplined Attention

Enduring constant distraction is ubiquitous in our lives today, but the ability to command unwavering attention is a refined leadership skill. Disciplined attention declutters chaos and encourages precise clarity. At Apple, this principle is embodied in the relentless pursuit of simplicity. Steve Jobs famously challenged his teams to "simplify, then simplify again," ruthlessly eliminating extraneous features and distractions to create products that command attention through sheer elegance and focus.

Steven Hobfoll defined resource allocation theory in the 1980s based on the premise that individuals have finite personal resources (e.g., time, energy, attention) that must be strategically allocated to achieve desired outcomes. A central tenet of this theory is the principle of conservation of resources, which posits that people are motivated to acquire, protect, and nurture resources valuable to them. Resource allocation theory highlights several key points:

- Attention is a limited cognitive resource that leaders must carefully manage and allocate across competing demands and priorities.
- Effective leaders recognize that unfocused attention leads to resource depletion, diminishing productivity and performance. They proactively structure the work environment to minimize distractions and interruptions that tax attentional resources.
- By setting clear priorities, leaders signal to their teams where to focus attentional resources for maximum impact. Regular progress reviews reinforce this focus.
- Leaders foster a culture of accountability by encouraging time management practices and self-regulation of attention. This cultivates disciplined attention as an organizational norm.
- Providing adequate resources (e.g. staffing, tools, training) prevents attentional overload that can lead to burnout and performance degradation.

Yet, focus alone is not enough. True leaders must actively cultivate an environment that nurtures and protects this precious resource. They establish clear priorities, set specific, measurable goals and regularly review progress to keep their teams aligned. They minimize distractions, providing guidelines on task importance and fostering a culture of accountability and time management.

While at Accenture, I focused on transforming talent

management to better suit our current climate, incorporating design elements that promote this goal. This initiative was largely inspired by Microsoft's efforts to overhaul its performance management system, aiming to reduce detrimental competition among employees and encourage a more cooperative atmosphere.

Previously, Microsoft employed a controversial "stack ranking" system that forced managers to grade employees against one another on a rigid curve, designating a portion as underperformers. This approach bred an overly competitive culture detrimental to teamwork and innovation. Microsoft abolished stack ranking in favor of a more flexible system focused on individual growth and development. The new process includes setting personal goals, maintaining performance journals for continuous feedback, and conducting frequent check-ins rather than high-stakes annual reviews. Employees receive a single rating tied to their contributions, behaviors, and capabilities, which determines their compensation increases without pitting them against peers. By removing forced rankings and enabling more frequent coaching conversations, Microsoft aimed to reduce excessive internal competition and promote a culture of shared success.

Competition is tied to the work of Steven Hobfoll around resource allocation and the conservation of resources. Competition within organizations can be detrimental as it leads to a depletion of valuable resources. The theory posits that individuals strive to acquire, protect, and maintain resources, which include objects, personal characteristics, conditions, or energies. When competition for limited resources intensifies, it creates a scarcity mindset, leading to increased stress levels and resource depletion. A study by Gorgievski and Hobfoll (2008) found that in highly competitive work environments, employees experienced a 27% higher rate of burnout compared to those in less competitive settings.

Furthermore, a meta-analysis by Halbesleben et al. (2014) revealed that resource depletion due to competition was associated with a 16% decrease in job performance and a 22% increase in counterproductive work behaviors. Consequently, excessive competition within organizations can undermine collaboration, erode social support networks, and ultimately hinder overall productivity and well-being, as individuals become preoccupied with securing and protecting their resources at the expense of collective goals.

The ability to maintain disciplined attention amidst constant distraction is a critical leadership skill that drives clarity and productivity. Resource allocation theory underscores the importance of strategically managing limited cognitive resources like attention. Effective leaders mitigate resource depletion by structuring environments that minimize distractions and foster disciplined attention.

Microsoft's shift from a competitive stack ranking system to a collaborative performance management approach further exemplifies the need to protect resources from internal competition, promoting a culture of shared success. Ultimately, leaders who prioritize focused attention and resource conservation cultivate environments where both individuals and organizations can thrive.

Giving Work Back to the People

As mentioned earlier, the decreasing availability of experienced leaders combined with the rapid pace of industry advancements necessitates expanding our focus beyond our leaders. Driving ownership and execution at every level of the organization is a requirement to compete. Organizations thrive or struggle based on the displays of initiative and ownership of their workforce. Successful leaders catalyze this invaluable asset by empowering employees - granting autonomy, instilling confidence, and fostering a sense of purpose. This empowerment, if executed properly, results in exponential gains: Competent employees, emboldened by self-determination, perceive their work as genuinely impactful. Meaningfulness breeds engagement, driving proactive innovation and relentless contribution to organizational success.

To promote this transformative force, leaders must take decisive action:

- **Provide Resources:** Equip teams with the tools, data, and support required for effective execution.
- **Encourage Collaboration:** Cultivate an environment of cooperation, enabling employees to secure the synergies

needed to accomplish objectives.

- **Build Trust:** Strengthen organizational cohesion by demonstrating confidence in employees' abilities.

Empowered employees embody four dimensions:
- **Competence:** Confidence in their abilities.
- **Self-Determination:** Resiliency over obstacles.
- **Meaningfulness:** Alignment with values and goals.
- **Impact:** Believing their efforts create positive change.

Empowerment is more than a strategy - it drives initiative, and fuels sustained success. When empowered individuals with high self-efficacy pursue difficult goals, they invest more effort, persist longer, and develop better strategies. For example, a meta-analysis by Llorente-Alonso et al. (2023) found that psychological empowerment had a strong positive correlation (r=0.52) with intrinsic motivation, demonstrating how empowerment can enhance drive and performance when tackling challenging objectives. This combination of goals, self-belief, and empowerment enables individuals to achieve at higher levels.

Protecting Voices of Leadership from Below

To the degree that leaders can enable employees to not only survive, but to thrive differentiates the industry titans from the rest of the pack. Lifting marginalized voices, while inspiring divergent thinking requires a substantial amount of nurturing. First, employees must feel Safe—free from fears of retribution, ridicule, or being diminished. Psychological safety is a shared belief that the team is safe for interpersonal risk-taking. This is crucial for fostering an inclusive environment where diverse opinions are valued. Teams with high psychological safety are more innovative and perform better because members feel comfortable sharing ideas without fear of ridicule (Edmondson, 1999). One slip in integrity will result in extended periods of necessary repair to instill trust.

Secondly, feeling like you matter is important. Employees must believe they have the necessary skills to contribute meaningfully to drive value. Further, employees must see the role they play and the tasks and products they deliver as being integral to the ultimate success of the organization. Feeling valued and knowing that one matters in the workplace significantly boosts motivation and performance by fostering a sense of purpose. When employees perceive their contributions and tasks as meaningful and appreciated, they are more engaged, committed, and productive.

Leaders who reinforce the complexity of the task, while also instilling their confidence in employees will inevitably derive greater productivity. Difficult and specific goals, when combined with a strong sense of self-efficacy, can drive higher performance. Challenging goals focus attention, mobilize effort, increase persistence, and motivate strategy development. However, goals alone are insufficient - self-efficacy provides the confidence to expend effort and persist through obstacles.

Thirdly, belonging in the workplace is crucial for harnessing insights, enhancing performance, and ensuring organizational success. Employees who feel a sense of belonging are more engaged, leading to higher productivity, better performance, and lower turnover rates (Gallup, 2017). Workplaces that foster belonging benefit from the unique perspectives of diverse teams, driving innovation and problem-solving (Catalyst, 2013). Research shows that belonging is key to leveraging diversity and improving performance. By creating an inclusive culture, building psychological safety, and promoting engagement, organizations can ensure all employees feel valued and empowered, driving overall success.

Lastly, being cherished by others for unique individual characteristics can be a changemaker. Leaders who value and cherish the unique characteristics of their employees can unlock unparalleled levels of productivity, dedication, and resiliency. This involves not only making employees feel safe for their divergent ideas, background, and experiences, but seeking to include those thoughts. If one feels valued for their unique thoughts, they will not only believe they are necessary, but feel a sense of ownership in the outcome.

Leaders play a crucial role in fostering an environment that encourages divergent thoughts and elevates voices. By creating a safe and inclusive culture, promoting open communication, empowering employees, facilitating collaboration, and recognizing contributions, leaders can unlock the full potential of their team's diverse perspectives. This not only drives innovation, but also strengthens organizational resilience and competitive advantage.

Building Trust: The Foundation of Influence and Effectiveness

Trust stands as the absolute pinnacle and foundation of all leadership greatness. It is the indispensable currency that fuels collaboration, ignites engagement, and propels performance. At its core, trust is the willingness to render ourselves vulnerable, strengthened by the positive expectations we hold regarding another's intentions and actions. It is a belief in that person's reliability, integrity, and competence – a belief that must be earned through consistent behavior and shared values.

Nontrivial impacts of strong trust include:

Collaboration

When trust permeates a team, barriers dissolve. Ideas flow freely, risks are embraced, and a synergistic force emerges, driving collective efforts towards common goals.

Engagement

Under the guidance of trustworthy leaders, employees feel valued, safe, and empowered. This promotes unparalleled engagement, job satisfaction, and an inextinguishable motivation to excel.

Amplified Performance

Trust liberates teams from excessive control, enabling autonomy and empowerment to thrive. Productivity soars as innovation is enabled, fueled by the confidence that employees can execute with excellence.

Conflicts Resolved

Where trust is strong, even the most formidable conflicts find resolution. Parties engage in constructive dialogue, seeking mutually beneficial solutions, united by a shared belief in each other's good intentions.

Yet, trust remains an elusive pursuit for many organizations. Gallup's sobering 2023 findings reveal that a mere 23% of employees strongly trust their leaders, a stark reminder of the work that lies ahead.

To cultivate trust, we must understand its components. Mayer and colleagues (1999) highlight that trust is dynamic and evolves through repeated interactions, influenced by factors such as inherent trust propensity, personality traits, and past experiences. Positive, consistent behaviors by leaders enhance trust, while negative experiences or inconsistencies erode it. By examining interactions and understanding an employee's history and trust levels, leaders can rebuild and strengthen trust within their teams.

I propose focusing on the following four pillars of trust:

Reliability: A steadfast dependability, honoring commitments and maintaining consistent, predictable behavior.

- Establish Service Level Agreements (SLAs) and engage in expectation setting.
- Communicate early when timelines are in jeopardy.
- Keep promises, meet deadlines, and maintain a predictable presence.

Competence: A mastery of skills and knowledge, inspiring confidence in one's ability to deliver successful outcomes.

- Continuous learning, skill development, and professional behavior.
- Synthesize and operationalize complexity.
- Consult Early and Align Often: Ensure requirements are agreed and deliver an acceptable solution.

Empathy: A genuine concern for others, a belief that one's interests are prioritized, and emotional needs are understood.

- Seek to find the greater good from diverse sets of team members.
- Respect and receive input from others that disagree with you.
- Lift up others! Show genuine care.
- Advocate for other teams and employees.

Integrity: An unwavering adherence to moral principles, ethical conduct, and a commitment to fairness and transparency.

- Demonstrate ethical behavior, fairness, and honesty.
- Demonstrate emotional stability and equanimity.
- Show authenticity and vulnerability.
- Communicate lavishly in good times and bad.
- Share information, explain decisions, and be transparent about intentions.

By consciously fortifying trust through deliberate actions, leaders can build enduring relationships foundational for influence. As a leader in the HR space, I frequently address interpersonal conflicts in the workplace, acting as an advisor to leaders and executives. My approach often begins with analyzing behavioral patterns against the components of trust. This framework allows for the swift identification of improvement areas and the alleviation of frustrations.

One of the challenges a client experienced involved peers and team members frequently bypassing him, undermining his influence and participation. During my coaching, we worked to evaluate each of the four pillars of trust. Although the executive was well-respected and a subject matter expert, his high standards and heavy workload often led to impatience and occasional negativity. We discussed how employees can avoid interacting with leaders who display negative emotions to protect their own well-being and reduce stress.

By focusing on "assuming good intent" and adopting behaviors that encouraged "getting curious with compassion," we began to dismantle these barriers. We emphasized behaviors that could develop into habits, helping the executive resist the urge to rush to problem-solving without engaging others.

Similarly, the Trust model proves effective when consulting with executives on corporate culture. In addressing a cultural struggle within a startup, I crafted interview questions around the Trust construct. Employees felt that the relationship with their leaders was imbalanced and untrusting. They perceived a trend where leaders asked them to make sacrifices for the team and the company without reciprocating that same level of concern for their well-being.

Leaders must advocate for their employees as much as the company's success. This means acknowledging the efforts of team members, supporting their individual needs, and respecting their rational self-interests. When the relationship becomes one-sided, trust inevitably suffers. Leaders must demonstrate concern and respect by reciprocating support, ensuring both employees and leaders give and receive in equal measure. This balance is essential for maintaining robust, trust-based relationships within any organization.

Trust is essential for effective leadership for several reasons. It enhances collaboration by fostering relationships where team members feel comfortable sharing ideas, taking risks, and working together towards common goals. Trustworthy leaders create an environment of safety and value, leading to increased employee engagement, job satisfaction, and motivation.

Additionally, trust reduces the need for excessive monitoring and control, allowing for greater autonomy and empowerment, which in turn boosts productivity and innovation. Furthermore, trust aids in conflict resolution by encouraging constructive dialogue and the pursuit of mutually beneficial solutions.

Cultivating a Culture of Visionary Thinking

Visionary leadership involves thinking big while inspiring others to see and work towards a compelling future. Leaders play an integral role in nurturing and selecting creative ideas within their teams. Leaders must balance enthusiasm for new projects with practical considerations, ensuring initiatives remain on time and within budget. Effective leaders also address interpersonal issues and critically evaluate the feasibility of creative ideas, promoting collective creativity with healthy team dynamics.

Two divergent concepts of leadership are transformational and transactional leadership. It is helpful to compare transformational and transactional behaviors to uncover the differences between managing performance and inspiring creativity.

Transformational leadership is characterized by several key behaviors (Rafferty & Griffin, 2004):

Articulating a Vision: express an idealized vision of the future based on organizational values.

Inspirational Communication: deliver positive and encouraging messages that build motivation and confidence.

Supportive Leadership: show concern for followers and consider their needs.

Intellectual Stimulation: enhance employees' interest in problems and encourage innovative thinking.

Individualized Consideration: acknowledge and praise individual efforts towards achieving goals.

In contrast, transactional leadership focuses on:

Contingent Reward: Providing support and resources in exchange for performance.

Active Management by Exception: Monitoring performance and taking corrective action as needed.

Passive Management by Exception: Intervening only when problems become severe.

Laissez-faire Leadership: Avoiding leadership responsibilities altogether.

Driving visionary thinking and creativity is inspired by transformational leaders and is a competitive advantage for fostering a culture of innovation, adaptability, and long-term success within organizations. By emphasizing culture and driving execution, leaders can promote conditions that inspire inventive solutions, capabilities and results.

Visionary thinking thrives in an environment that embraces uncertainty, where leaders are emboldened to ignore convention and fearlessly explore. Foster a culture that challenges the status quo, empowering yourself and others to question norms, defy conventional wisdom, and push boundaries. Fueling creativity necessitates high levels of patience, humility, acceptance, and encouragement to harness the benefits of diverse perspectives through cross-functional collaboration and inclusive environments. Confidence in oneself and great admiration for other team members are nontrivial to enable creative conditions. Nurture innovation by providing essential time for reflection, imagination, and free exploration.

Executing Visionary Thinking

Strategic thinkers often face criticism for their inability to execute their visions effectively. It's not enough to dream big; leaders must also execute with speed, skill, and sophistication. Within organizations, a natural tension exists between the urgency to act and the need for collaboration, where the principle "Go slow to go fast" becomes crucial. This concept urges leaders to invest time in thorough preparation and thoughtful consideration before diving into execution.

Early in my career, I evaluated the work requirements for parole agents, including employment, training criteria, and physical fitness documentation. This involved ride-alongs in areas like South Central Los Angeles and focus groups with supervisors and employees. I ensured transparency by involving union representatives at every stage and discussing their lives during lunches, building trust. This approach proved valuable during a tense meeting between union and management when a union representative defended my work. Through this process, I gained an influential advocate who helped champion the effort.

Turning visionary ideas into reality requires more than sheer determination; it demands a masterful execution strategy. A clear and compelling change mandate is essential to fully motivate employees, drive dedication, and reinforce resilience. Employees must deeply believe in the vision and align their efforts toward a shared, inspiring future.

Once this foundational alignment is in place, leaders must meticulously outline a rigorous, thoughtful, and optimistic path forward. Engaging stakeholders early to leverage collective wisdom is crucial. Continuous alignment with organizational goals necessitates frequent progress tracking and strategic recalibration.

Only through a sophisticated execution approach – fostering deep employee commitment, charting a well-defined roadmap, and maintaining steadfast organizational alignment – can visionary leaders transform ideas into impactful realities that shape the future. For instance, Apple and Tesla have demonstrated how a blend of visionary leadership and meticulous execution can revolutionize industries, emphasizing that success lies in the harmony of strategic thinking and flawless implementation.

Outlining a Clear Path Forward

Visionary leaders that chart a well-defined roadmap and a strategic blueprint precisely navigating the path from aspiration to achievement can drive greater collective achievements. This roadmap demands rigorous precision, detailed milestones, timelines, and measurable objectives that guide progress. Yet, it must also embody thoughtful foresight, proactively addressing potential obstacles, resource constraints, and contingencies that may arise.

Crucially, this visionary roadmap must radiate an aura of optimism, igniting hope and enthusiasm among stakeholders. It should paint a vivid, inspiring picture of the future, captivating hearts and minds, and rallying collective efforts towards a shared, transcendent goal. Only through this harmonious fusion of precision and inspiration can visionary leaders forge a roadmap that transforms dreams into reality.

Consulting Stakeholders Early

Visionary leaders rally stakeholders from the outset, harnessing collective insights to forge a unifying vision. Through early engagement with employees, customers, partners, and investors, they address concerns head-on and cultivate a groundswell of support. This collaborative approach aligns the vision with stakeholder needs and values, fostering buy-in while diminishing resistance to change that will need mitigating at every point of inflection.

A compelling example is Satya Nadella's transformation of Microsoft. Upon becoming CEO, Nadella consulted extensively with employees, partners, and customers, shaping his vision for a "mobile-first, cloud-first" company. This inclusive approach helped rally support and facilitated a successful cultural shift.

Ensuring Continuous Alignment

Visionary leaders relentlessly align execution with organizational imperatives. They vigilantly monitor progress, pivoting strategies when required. Consistent communication updates stakeholders, ensuring the vision's relevance to the mission, values, and objectives. This iterative cycle propels the organization toward realizing transformative ideas.

Research by McKinsey & Company highlights the importance of continuous alignment, finding that successful transformations involve ongoing monitoring, course-correction, and reinforcement of the change mandate. Companies that fail to maintain alignment often struggle to sustain momentum and achieve their visionary goals. They found that companies with strong alignment between strategy and execution are 2.2 times more likely to outperform their peers financially.

Practical examples of this can be seen throughout the tech industry. Consider a software development team that adopts Agile methodologies. By holding daily stand-up meetings, conducting regular sprint reviews, and fostering an environment of open communication, the team ensures that everyone is on the same page. This continuous alignment allows the team to swiftly adapt to changes, address issues promptly, and deliver high-quality products efficiently.

A Call to Embrace Disruption, Forge Trust, and Inspire Greatness

In this time of constant change and disruption, strong leadership is built by navigating uncertainty. It is a journey that demands an unwavering commitment to integrity, a steadfast dedication to building trust, and an unquenchable thirst for visionary thinking. To lead without being disruptive, we must embrace ambiguity as a catalyst for growth, thriving amidst the chaos by leveraging agility and resilience. We must cultivate environments where teams feel empowered to innovate, to challenge conventions, and to fearlessly pursue bold ideas.

Yet, true leadership extends far beyond mere adaptation – it is a selfless calling to inspire greatness in others for the greater good. By casting a compelling vision that resonates with the deepest aspirations of those we lead, we ignite a fire that sustains despite adversity and lead to collective success. Despite all the advances in technology and the increased demands on employees, trust remains the essential source that fuels collaboration, ignites engagement, and propels performance. It is an impact that must be cultivated through consistent behavior, ethical conduct, and genuine empathy.

The new C-Suite's future will be fraught with new challenges, but the rewards are immeasurable. For those who embrace disruption, forge trust, and inspire greatness, the likelihood of disruption without being a disruptor is enhanced – a testament to the indomitable spirit of visionary leadership.

Cast aside complacency and embrace the mantle of selfless leadership. Let us all be the architects of change, the beacons of trust, and the catalysts of visionary thinking, forever pushing the boundaries of what is possible and leaving our mark on those individuals that we lift around us.

The time is now, the stage is set – the future belongs to those who dare to lead.

About Dr. Deborah K. Ford

Organizational Psychology Expert & HR Consultant

Meet Dr. Deborah K. Ford, a leading expert in organizational psychology with over 20 years of experience in Human Resources. Armed with a Ph.D. from Portland State University and a Master's from George Mason University, Dr. Ford specializes in building high-performing teams and creating inclusive, innovative workplaces.

In her career, Dr. Ford has been the go-to consultant for Fortune 500 companies, especially in the fast-paced tech and AI sectors of Silicon Valley. Her deep knowledge of leadership development, change management, and cultural transformation has helped organizations gain a serious competitive edge.

Beyond consulting, Dr. Ford is a prolific author and speaker, sharing her expertise at international conferences, on podcasts, and through numerous book chapters, white papers, and academic articles. Her insights on talent management and leadership are widely respected in the industry.

Passionate about mentoring the next generation, Dr. Ford also serves as an executive coach at Wings for Growth, where she brings her expertise to life, helping leaders apply psychological and leadership principles in real-world scenarios.

Civil Leadership

By Tiana Sanchez

We Are in the People Business

A few years ago, I attended a conference in Long Beach, CA with a friend. Seated in the front row, I listened attentively to the keynote speaker. He spoke passionately about his organization and the transformative changes they were implementing to improve workplace culture.

The keynote speaker described a workplace where employees could take a break in the middle of the day to go surfing. At first, I found this unusual, but it intrigued me. He then shared that employees were allowed to bring their pets to work—something that was neither common nor trendy at the time.

He continued by explaining how the company supported new parents, offering childcare so they could bring their kids to work. As a working mother with two children, I would have greatly appreciated this incredible benefit.

What really impressed me was that the company matched employees' contributions to the causes they cared about. This innovative and supportive environment was none other than Patagonia.

When we hear the term "workplace culture," it can evoke various thoughts. You might picture a place where colleagues work in a toxic environment. Perhaps you envision an environment where work is enjoyable or, conversely, overwhelming. Maybe you think of a setting where leaders genuinely listen to and care about their employees' concerns. You might also imagine a culture guided by humanity, one that considers the pace of daily operations, accommodates working parents, and supports causes important to its employees. This was the kind of workplace culture the conference speaker discussed.

I had heard of Patagonia, though I had never shopped there. While I enjoy a range of activities, outdoor sports aren't my thing—I don't hike, cycle, or ski. Despite my lack of interest in these activities, I was aware that Patagonia was a brand that celebrated the outdoor lifestyle. Listening to the speaker on stage, however, left me thoroughly impressed. From that moment on, I seized every opportunity to share the story of this remarkable company.

In every meeting with my clients, I would ask, "Have you heard of Patagonia? Do you know what they do for their employees?" I would then share how parents could bring their children to work, thanks to on-site childcare. I would describe how employees could go hiking, swimming, or surfing in the middle of the day. Clients often looked at me skeptically, but they found it intriguing because no other company, to my knowledge, was doing anything like it. It was a novel and inspiring idea.

While I was enthusiastically sharing Patagonia's story to anyone who would listen, I found myself increasingly intrigued by the company. I realized there was something uniquely significant about their approach. They weren't just selling products like jackets and outdoor wear—they were promoting a sense of humanity and a genuine people-centric culture. They didn't just talk about it; they lived it.

In my exploration, I discovered something new: Patagonia was a Certified B Corporation. I was familiar with S Corps and C Corps, but this was the first time I had encountered a Certified B Corporation. Curious, I delved deeper to understand what this designation meant. According to the B Corporation website, a B Corp Certification is **"a designation that a business is meeting high standards of verified performance, accountability, and transparency on factors from employee benefits and charitable giving to supply chain**

practices and input materials". In order for a company to achieve certification, the company must meet these three overarching standards:

1. **Demonstrate high social and environmental performance** by achieving a B Impact Assessment score of 80 or above and passing our risk review. Multinational corporations must also meet baseline requirement standards.

2. **Make a legal commitment** by changing their corporate governance structure to be accountable to all stakeholders, not just shareholders, and achieve benefit corporation status if available in their jurisdiction.

3. **Exhibit transparency** by allowing information about their performance measured against B Lab's standards to be publicly available on their B Corp profile on B Lab's website.

My first thought was, "Why has no one ever told me about this?" As I delved deeper into B Corp Certification and learned about these impact areas, I couldn't help but wonder why more organizations weren't pursuing this. The answer, I believed, lay in the rigorous certification process of B Corporation, which evaluates a company across multiple dimensions, ensuring legal accountability to all stakeholders—workers, communities, customers, suppliers, and the environment—not just shareholders. A company must demonstrate commitment and determination, valuing the importance of undertaking this type of process. These multiple dimensions are referred to as Impact Areas.

The five Impact Areas of the B Impact Assessment (BIA) for Certified B Corporations include:

Governance: This evaluates a company's overall mission, engagement around social and environmental impact, code of ethics, and transparency. It ensures that the company's governance structure is accountable to all stakeholders, not just shareholders.

Workers: This assesses a company's treatment and benefits for its employees, including fair compensation, safe working conditions, and opportunities for professional development.

Community: This examines a company's impact on the local community, including charitable giving, volunteer programs, and community engagement.

Customers: This evaluates a company's treatment and services to its customers, including fair pricing, product quality, and customer support.

Environment: This assesses a company's environmental impact, including sustainable practices, waste reduction, and environmental stewardship.

These Impact Areas form the foundation of the BIA, where companies are evaluated and scored. This standardized framework helps businesses measure and manage their social and environmental performance effectively. It allows companies to:

Assess: Evaluate their current impact on stakeholders through 50-250 questions.

Compare: Review and compare their performance with thousands of other businesses.

Improve: Access customized reports, best practices, and resources to set and track performance goals.

The scoring in this assessment is unique. Any score above zero indicates that the company is making a positive impact on society and the environment. For instance, if a company regularly contributes to a charity or has a strategy for ethical employment practices, points are added to their score. A score of 80 or above is considered good, while the average score falls between 50 and 55.

This curiosity sparked my journey to understanding B Corp certification better and how many other organizations held this designation. I wanted to support these organization and be well-informed for discussions with leaders, as these topics hadn't come up in my previous conversations.

After 20 years in business, working in various leadership roles across the public and private sectors—from food and beverage companies to banks and retail—I had never encountered a designation that signaled a company's commitment to a holistic standard of excellence. However, in 2020, due to the pandemic, I paused my research and exploration.

Things Changed in 2020

When 2020 hit, we saw the best and the worst of humanity. We saw a lot of leaders that were responding because they were in a crisis mode. There was widespread injustice and division, accompanied by confusion and concern in our society, which inevitably spilled over into our workplaces, affecting the people within our organizations.

From that crisis, people began to care more deeply. This was the best part of humanity. We were also careful about what we were saying, what we were doing, and about the conversations we were having. It awakened a new consciousness, an awareness of the reality of inequality that we hadn't seen before or perhaps that we chose to overlook. It brought to light a reality that some of us may have previously chosen to ignore, but now we couldn't avoid it because it was right there in front of us. That shifted the culture in our organizations, and we started to change.

Companies began implementing training initiatives in their organizations to advocate for diversity, equity, inclusion, and justice. New programs, departments, and positions were created, and people were hired to drive these efforts. Company leaders felt proud, confident that they were doing the right thing for the right reasons. Chief Diversity and Chief People Officers were hired. Company leaders made statements of solidarity and participated in peaceful demonstrations. They advocated for justice, fairness, and equity and pushed back against broken systems that were contrary to those beliefs. Again, everyone felt like they were doing the right thing for the right reasons. There was a collective momentum felt across the country, and at my company, TSI, LLC, we experienced it as well.

2020 Growth in Crises

At the beginning of 2020, while other companies were expanding programs and growing their workforce, our firm was growing too. Looking back at how we performed, we anticipated matching the previous year's profits. However, by March, like many other consultancy firms, we experienced a dip in sales and expected to see a loss by year's end as sales continued to trend downward. This decline lasted until June. But from July through October, sales surged as companies increasingly sought our training and coaching services, our two top sellers. We started the year expecting to break even, then braced for a loss, and ultimately ended up doubling our sales! It was quite a ride, marked by great tragedy and uncertainty.

The following year, in 2021, we doubled our sales once again. In 2022, sales increased by 22%, followed by a 13% increase in 2023. Over a span of four years, our revenue surged by 454%. This increase was directly attributed to the global pandemic and the civil unrest. Companies acted with urgency to engage firms like mine to develop and facilitate programs. Additionally, those companies transitioning from in-person to remote-first operations sought assistance in teaching managers how to lead effectively in this new environment. During this period, we developed and facilitated dozens of training programs, both virtually and in person, training hundreds if not thousands of employees. We designed, developed, and administered surveys, assessments, and diversity audits across a diverse range of organizations, from entertainment to aerospace.

From those early revenue spurts that occurred between July and October, I wanted to bring all our learnings, team efforts, and experiences to the forefront. By the end of 2020, I published a whitepaper titled "The Awakening: The Rise of the Conscious Leader." This whitepaper served as a call to action for leaders, providing guidance on how to adopt more ethical and equitable leadership practices. It featured a 7-step schematic, essentially outlining what leaders need to do in their organizations to ensure they are doing what's right for the right reasons.

A. Racial/Gender Equity Commitment

Conscious leaders must define and formalize the commitment to actively pursue racial and gender equity. It is not enough just to think it, know it, practice it, and preach it. It must be codified. Naturally, an internal policy reorganization may be required.

B. Core Values

Conscious leaders must reevaluate and/or establish core values through an equity lens. How does one do that? To start, ask the tough questions. Sometimes just raising the questions alone can bring about necessary awareness and further discussions on equity.

C. Sustaining Equity

Once extant, equity must be maintained. What tools can a conscious leader deploy in that regard? From employee-resource/ affinity groups to venues, spaces, programs, and other internal offerings, conscious leaders can turn virtually any forum into a mechanism to reinforce equity. It's all about their perspective, awareness, and creativity.

D. Training

Conscious leaders rely heavily on data and analysis-driven formalized training. Guessing never cuts it. So, choosing training methodology based on a limited or skewed perspective will never do either. Honesty, objectivity, analysis, and self-awareness are the starting point for conscious leaders designing or facilitating training. As previously mentioned, "training is a wholly supportive measure weaved into an established corporate infrastructure." Formalization and institutionalization of training is key, but so is oversight, accountability, measurement, and evaluation.

E. Equity Work

Conscious leaders rely on two elements to ensure an equitable work environment. They are restorative practices and equitable representation.

1) Restorative Practices: A social science that studies how to improve and repair relationships between people and communities.

2) Equitable Representation: community diversification in education, local government, and business ownership that directly affects where we live and work.

F. Disparities

Again, honesty counts. But so do perception and analysis. Conscious leaders must recognize disparities within an organization and position themselves to do something meaningful about it.

G. Resistance

Resistance is anything but futile. It's often present and can be a considerable obstacle. Conscious leaders must stand firm in their commitment, repelling external pressures and staying true to their convictions.

One key insight from our research, inspired by McKinsey's Agile Organizational Perspective, is that organizations should operate more like organisms than machines. An organism is a living, breathing entity—and we, as individuals, embody this concept. However, we often treat our workplaces like machines, especially in an era dominated by AI and automation. This model offers a refreshing perspective, urging us to shift away from mechanistic operations and view organizations as living entities.

However, much of that progress is changing now, and we're witnessing some regression. The awakening and heightened consciousness of 2020 had leaders responding to crises with curiosity and accountability. Now, we are encountering similar issues, but responding in vastly different ways. Welcome to 2024.

The War on DEI

The crisis we're seeing within organizations reflects a shift from once declaring the necessity of equitable and ethical work to defunding it. Diversity, equity, and inclusion, which we once held close as essential values, are being dismissed. Instead of championing these principles for the benefit of our people, we are beginning to weaponize this language in our environments.

Between September 2019 and September 2020, job postings for diversity, inclusion and belonging rose 56.3%. (Murray) The patterns of C-Suite roles changed significantly during this time. Four C-suite titles have seen significant hiring growth since 2019: Chief Diversity and Inclusion Officer (+168.9%), Chief Delivery Officer (+165.6%), Chief People Officer (+144.3%), and Chief Growth Officer (+117.5%).

Remarkably, less than two years later, we observed a decline in these roles. (Donegan) According to a LinkedIn study, the hiring of

Chief Diversity Officers decreased by 4.51% in 2022, despite being the fastest-growing title in 2020 and 2021.

The rapid movement of organizations to address this particular crisis was fast and furious. Many companies over promised and under delivered on their commitments. As a result, we are now seeing these programs disappear.

The tech industry has been significantly impacted by mass layoffs, with a disproportionate number of DEI positions being eliminated. According to Crunchbase, a comprehensive platform with company insights and trends, "more than 191,000 workers in the U.S.-based tech companies (or tech companies with a large U.S. workforce) were laid off in mass job cuts in 2023." At least 54,343 workers were laid off in 2024. ("Tech Layoffs: US Companies With Job Cuts In and 2023 and 2024")

Now there's a new crisis that leaders are responding to - the war on DEI. Really, it's a war on our humanity and our civility toward others. Leaders once emphasized the importance of this work, but now many are showing through their actions that they no longer care to prioritize it. Leaders previously conveyed the importance of psychological safety, promoting their companies as "safe spaces to speak up." This demonstration of de-prioritizing DEI work may cause employees to feel uneasy or apprehensive. They may fear that saying the wrong thing or speaking up for what they believe is right could jeopardize their job security. The consciousness we developed as a society often feels undermined, which could leave many of us feeling conned.

What once seemed crucial now appears less important, as our culture increasingly tolerates cuts to training programs, costs, and positions. The roles we declared vital three years ago have been eliminated, and programs and departments we established have been defunded and dismantled. As a result, the culture itself has been cut, and layoffs have surged. This situation reminds me of a game of Jenga—removing critical pieces, one by one, until the structure becomes unstable and collapses. Are we willing to accept a "Jenga-like" business model? I'm not.

The Jenga Business Model

Have you ever played Jenga? I have two boys, and we used to play Jenga together when they were kids. It wasn't my favorite game, primarily because the blocks inevitably topple. I always anticipated the moment they would fall and the loud noise that would follow. The purpose of Jenga, a word that means "to build," is to stack blocks as high as possible. You and a partner take turns pulling pieces from the bottom of the stack and placing them on top, trying not to make the structure fall. You continue this process, building the structure higher and higher until it eventually collapses.

This game mirrors our approach to culture, especially in a

capitalistic society that emphasizes rapid growth and high revenue. We focus on building quickly and growing tall, much like stacking blocks in Jenga, aiming to reach greater heights. We're just stacking. And when we get to a certain point, we realize, OK, I need to grow a little bit higher. What am I going to do? I'm going to take a little piece from the bottom. I'm going to remove that piece and place it on top. So now I'm cutting. I'm pulling from things that I thought were important just to continue that growth. I'm pulling from our funding. I'm pulling from our employees. I'm taking necessary things just so that I can grow high and grow big.

What happens to the foundation when we keep pulling from the bottom? It starts to shake. It starts to become unstable. It starts to crumble. Many organizations now have shaky, unstable foundations, on the verge of toppling because they sacrificed core elements in their pursuit of growth and revenue. I believe we need to move away from the Jenga approach. Instead, I challenge us to think more like Lego builders.

The Legos Business Model

It feels less like a game and more like a focused activity on creation. Legos represent creativity and collaboration. It's not just about growing tall but also about growing wide, involving people and resources. With Legos, your imagination is limitless. How many of you know that with Legos, you have different colors, sizes, and shapes? You can involve so many people in the process, making it a diverse and inclusive activity.

When we talk about Legos, something else that comes to mind is the connection with Star Wars. Star Wars is iconic, and every year, people worldwide celebrate May 4th with the greeting, "May the 4th be with you." On May 4th, 2024, Downtown Disney unveiled a massive Star Wars Lego mural. Guests were given a Lego square with a number on the back, indicating where to place it on the mural. Over the course of three days, hundreds of people participated, adding thousands of pieces to the mural. Star Wars fans from various locations and backgrounds came together to create a beautiful, collaborative work of art.

I believe this Lego approach exemplifies building not just upward but also outward. These creations involved significant time, resources, and collaboration from many people, all while maintaining their creativity. They didn't compromise their end goal by taking from one area to build higher. Instead, they worked together to create something expansive and inclusive.

Civil-led Leadership

Reflecting on our cultural evolution, it's clear that we often operate in crisis mode. Our leaders are typically driven by crises, reacting to issues that, while they may spark a heightened level of care and awareness, often lead us to address problems we ignored or hadn't previously recognized.

I propose that we shift from a crisis-driven mindset to a civility-driven mindset. Instead of allowing crises to dictate our actions and guide our work, we should focus on fostering a civil-led approach in our organizations and leadership teams. This approach reflects humanity, a humaneness, in the work we do—reminiscent of Patagonia's approach.

As we strive to elevate our awareness and improve our workplaces, holding our leaders to a higher standard of leadership, I want to introduce three key concepts to you. But first, let me define Civil Leadership.

In this context, Civil Leadership means aligning community, social responsibility, and individual creativity, connecting business principles with global initiatives for longevity and sustainability.

In a civil mindset and leadership approach, we examine our traditional paradigms and business models and acknowledge they are not good enough. We challenge the conventional shareholder capitalistic ideals, striving to do better. Traditional shareholder capitalism prioritized revenue over people, and we must challenge this mindset within organizations.

Take Boeing, for instance. Boeing is a multi-billion-dollar global aerospace company that develops, manufactures and services commercial airplanes, defense products and space systems for customers in more than 150 countries. In March 2024 a door panel blew off mid-flight on a Boeing 737 Max 9 aircraft that took off from Portland, Oregon. A federal inquiry into Boeing's safety measures revealed that the day before take-off, engineers and technicians were concerned over a safety light that indicated an issue with the plane's pressurization system. (Sorace) Investigators also found that four bolts were missing from the door panel. You might be wondering the same thing as me: HOW COULD SOMETHING LIKE THIS HAPPEN?

From the outside looking in, it appears as though their leadership prioritized speed over quality, leading to significant scrutiny from the National Transportation Safety Board (NTSB) and the Federal Aviation Administration (FAA). According to a six-week review by the FAA, Boeing's manufacturing processes for the 737 Max failed 33 out of 89 aspects, as reported by The New York Times. (Nerozzi) It later emerged that Boeing employees had raised concerns about certain issues but were ignored or not taken seriously. When employee's express hesitation to use the very products they help create, it's a clear red flag.

If you look at these events externally, it would seem like company leaders have sacrificed humanity, quality, and essential values for profit. Challenging these outdated mindsets and models requires us to embrace a new approach to leadership and work. It's time to prioritize people and quality, fostering a more humane and ethical business environment.

Key Concept #1: Community First

Community First embodies a Servant Leadership approach, signifying, "I'm here to serve you." If you place your hands out in front of you with your palms up, it looks like you're waiting for someone to give you something, conveying a "give me, give me, give me" attitude. Now, turn your hands so your palms face down or outward. This gesture says, "I want to give to you." A community-first mindset is about having palms down, ready to give rather than receive.

Some people might argue that this approach will sacrifice business metrics like profitability. However, a 2020 research study analyzing 55 stores in France found that Servant Leadership positively influenced both revenue and profits through increased employee engagement. (Percy)

If we wish to lead with a community-first mind-set and take a Servant Leadership approach, we need to ask ourselves the following questions:

How do you prioritize serving your team over seeking personal recognition or benefits within your leadership approach?
- Can you provide an example of a time when you made a decision that primarily benefited your employees or the community, even if it didn't directly benefit you?
- How do you demonstrate empathy and understanding in

your daily interactions with your team members?

- In what ways do you actively support and encourage the personal and professional growth of your employees?
- How do you foster an inclusive environment where every team member feels valued and heard?
- Can you describe a situation where you put the needs of your team or organization above your own, and what was the outcome?
- How do you balance the demands of achieving organizational goals while maintaining a focus on the well-being and development of your employees?
- Do you embody the principles of Servant Leadership by prioritizing integrity, ethics, and humility while serving a higher purpose within the organization?
- Do you tend to put people first, demonstrating care and support for employees' growth and goals?
- Do you frequently effectively communicate by listening, speaking, and soliciting feedback from the team?
- Are you a compassionate collaborator, fostering relationships, supporting diversity and inclusion, and navigating workplace conflicts?
- Do you tend to lead with moral authority, building trust through setting high standards, delegating responsibility, and fostering a culture of accountability within the workforce?

Key Concept #2: Collective Social Responsibility

Your willingness to contribute to society and the welfare of others involves taking action and being accountable for practices that benefit society. This includes environmental, political, volunteering, and social causes. Some refer to this as setting ESG (Environmental, Social, and Governance) goals, while others call it corporate social responsibility. I prefer the term "collective social responsibility" because it involves everyone—from frontline staff to the CEO, community members, policymakers, legal teams, and businesses of all sizes. Every one of us has a social responsibility to each other because when one of us thrives, we all thrive.

A 2023 study by Stanford reveals that only about 16% of US organizations adopt social responsibility as a value compared to more than 50 percent of companies in Germany, France, Belgium and Canada. (Kiger and Reichelstein) Socially responsible organizations improve corporate culture by attracting talent and creating goodwill with the public and potential customers. Social responsibility is becoming increasingly important among millennials and the younger generation.

Key Concept #3: Creative Synthesis

Lastly, there's what we call creative synthesis, which involves blending everyone's ideas, unique perspectives, and elements to create something new. Think of it this way: when making a smoothie, you have different ingredients—strawberries, blueberries, a banana, and some milk. Each ingredient has its own identity, character, and flavor, and each is delicious on its own.

When you blend them together, you create something unique and novel. Similarly, creative synthesis means embracing diverse perspectives and ideas, merging them to build something new and innovative. By valuing and incorporating diversity, we create something greater than the sum of its parts.

As we introduce these three new concepts representing civil leadership in action, let's focus on creativity: expanding outward like Legos, not just upward like Jenga. We're moving away from viewing organizations as machines and instead seeing them as living, breathing organisms.

When thinking about this shift, I envision a garden as the ideal workplace. I was not blessed with a green thumb, and although I'm not a gardener I love visiting gardens. In a garden there's no competitiveness—trees aren't trying to outgrow each other. Instead, you see a variety of plants and flowers, each unique and thriving in their own way. This diversity and harmony is what I want my workplace to emulate.

When I look at a garden, I envision what our workplaces could be.

What does it take to maintain a garden? It requires someone to care for it—a gardener. The gardener is the nurturer, the keeper of the garden, ensuring everything is well-maintained. They plant seeds, nurture growth, remove weeds, and continually cultivate the garden. This role is comparable to our leaders.

Additionally, we have the landscape. A garden's landscape is vast and wide, not just tall. This represents our corporate responsibility, where we oversee and care for the broader environment and community.

Let's also consider the sunlight and the environment, nurturing our garden. The roots go deep, symbolizing our vision, mission, and core values. All these elements work together harmoniously. If we envision our workplace as a garden with multiple thriving sections, each part contributes to the overall health and success.

By viewing our organizations less as machines and more like gardens, we embrace the concept of civil leadership in action, connecting our business with the broader world in a harmonious way. This shift requires our leaders to adapt. Inspired by the B Corp certification and its pillars, to facilitate this shift, I've developed ten guiding principles for you to explore which we will look at in the next section.

Civil Leadership in Action

At this point in the chapter, I want to highlight what we need to do as leaders. We understand how important this work is, and now it's time to take action and commit to practicing it for the long term. First, I've identified 10 principles that we need to adopt as civil leaders:

1. Leaders need to look beyond traditional business paradigms and envision new possibilities.
2. Leaders should consider all aspects of the business, not just the bottom line.
3. Leaders have a duty to act in the best interests of society at large.
4. Leaders should actively participate in community and societal affairs.
5. Leaders must be able to adapt to changing norms and expectations.
6. Leaders should uphold high moral standards in all their actions.
7. Leaders should foster an environment where diverse perspectives are valued and encouraged.
8. Leaders should strive to make a significant positive impact through their actions.
9. Leaders have the ability to shape and influence the culture of their organization.
10. Leaders should aim for success that is sustainable in the

long term, considering both environmental and business factor.

This list is not exhaustive but serves as a starting point. It's the beginning of a journey to build broadly and to nurture processes that sustain a world where business and the environment are interconnected.

Be in the Business of our Planet

A few years ago, I made a conscious decision to ensure that 80% of what I wore, every makeup product I used, my shoes, and household items were purchased from either a small-owned business, a Black-owned business, or a woman-owned business.

This decision was part of my commitment to supporting businesses within my community. While I could easily shop at Target, Nordstrom, or other high-end stores, I wanted to direct my support to smaller, minority-owned, and women-owned businesses.

So, I started searching online, and let me tell you, it's quite a process. It's not easy to find these companies, but with some diligent Googling, it's possible. It takes time and effort. I spent hours at the computer, searching to find these companies. If they didn't have a physical storefront, I would make my purchase online. This deliberate approach not only supports these businesses but also aligns with my values of ethical and responsible consumption.

The question that constantly weighed on my mind was: If not me, then who? And if not now, then when?

Around the same time, our family decided to focus more on reducing our carbon footprint by being mindful of our purchases. We switched to using bamboo tissue, which is supposed to be better for the environment. We minimized the number of chemical products in our home, opting for more natural alternatives. Additionally, we stopped using paper towels. I haven't used paper towels in about three years. Instead, we use something called "UN paper towels," which are reusable cloths. This choice was driven by our desire to reduce environmental impact.

These are intentional decisions that our family holds ourselves accountable for. As I introduce this level of accountability, it's important to recognize that it falls on your shoulders, as a leader, to commit to these practices. We must actively embody the change we want to see.

Stop Talking. Start Doing!

We need to stop talking about what we are going to do and do it. In the United States, and according to the US Census Bureau, there are between 6 and 7 million companies. Of these, about 95% to 98%

have fewer than 100 employees. (Small Business & Entrepreneurship Council) Now, consider this: only about 2,300 companies in the U.S. are certified B Corps, as of the writing of this chapter.

Out of 6 million companies, roughly 2,300 have undergone rigorous assessment and evaluation to prove they are doing things the right way for their community and organization, indicating a significant opportunity for growth in this area. Imagine if we could increase that number to even 1% of the total—60,000 companies.

Now, from a global perspective. According to Statista, the number of companies worldwide at the end of 2021 was 333 million. (Dyvik) According to B Lab's 2023 Annual Report, there are roughly 8,051 certified B Corporations worldwide. Clearly, this data presents a massive opportunity for leaders.

As a global community, we must move beyond just talking about it—we need to take action. If you are not in the C-Suite, you might be wondering, "What can I do? I'm not running the company; I don't have that level of influence. How can I get my leaders to care about the community and make better decisions for the benefit of our community? How can I help my company change old business practices and focus more on the community? What can I do to help lead this charge for my organization?"

There is a lot you can do. I'll give you five actionable steps to help your leaders care more about these issues, understand their impact, and perhaps even consider achieving B Corp status. Here are five things you can do right now:

Facilitate a Global Ethical Leadership Exchange

What does this mean in practice? Facilitate exchanges with leaders from other countries and cultures known for their ethical and socially responsible business practices, promoting cross-cultural learning and innovation.

Offer Community Sabbaticals

Offer sabbaticals for leaders to work with non-profits or community organizations, gaining firsthand experience in social responsibility and bringing back insights to integrate into the business.

Organize a Social Ethics Event

Organize a social event focused on solving ethical dilemmas and social issues, encouraging leaders to think creatively and collaboratively about integrating social responsibility into business strategies. Creating a forum for these conversations—whether once or twice a year—where organizations of all sizes can come together will spark meaningful exchanges. This starts a conversation and sets a precedent for other companies to follow. By addressing the challenges at hand, we can make decisions that benefit everyone.

Establish Ethical Innovation Labs

Set up dedicated labs within the company where leaders can experiment with new business models and practices focused on ethical innovation and community impact. This allows for more innovation in solving global and local issues within our community and company.

Create an Impact Investment Fund

Create a fund to support local social enterprises and community projects, with leaders involved in decision-making processes and fund management to foster a direct connection to social impact.

As you start down this path, you'll see that there's more opportunity and your imagination is limitless when you begin thinking less about yourself and more about the community at large.

A Vision for the Future

Civil leadership in action requires us to challenge traditional business models of shareholder capitalism. We need to start thinking of our workplaces as gardens and our leaders as gardeners—nurturing our environments.

We must hold our leaders accountable because we only have one planet to care for, and we must take care of our people as well. Moving away from a crisis-driven mindset, while maintaining awareness and consciousness, we should shift our culture to focus more on humanity and civility. This means treating each other with kindness and ensuring mutual thriving—if I thrive, you should thrive too.

Imagine a future where businesses thrive not just on profit margins but on human connection and community. In this landscape, workplaces prioritize culture, ethics, and social responsibility alongside financial success.

Picture leaders who embrace diversity and welcome varied perspectives, fostering an environment where every individual can flourish. Envision an organization as a vibrant garden, rooted in its values and nurtured by its leaders.

This is the vision for the future—a future where businesses flourish not only financially but also socially and ethically. Together, we can create a world where our organizations thrive in harmony with our communities and environment. Let this be our planet's legacy—a testament to our commitment to a better, more equitable future. This is just the beginning, and the path ahead is filled with endless possibilities. Let us walk this path with purpose and resolve, knowing that the future we envision is within our reach.

About Tiana Sanchez

CEO & Founder, TSI, LLC

Meet Tiana Sanchez, the dynamic CEO and Founder of TSI, LLC, a Woman-Owned Small Business with over a decade of experience as a Corporate Trainer and Business Consultant. Tiana is a #1 best-selling author and the voice behind a globally recognized podcast, earning her recognition for her insights, including a feature on KTLA Morning News for workplace empathy.

As an Award-Winning Executive Coach, Tiana leverages her diverse management experience across Aerospace, Tech, Media and Entertainment and Finance to elevate leadership and people development. Under her leadership, Tiana Sanchez International was named the "Best Executive Coaching" program by HR.Com, specializing in world-class leadership programs, keynotes, and seminars.

Tiana's expertise extends to Diversity Audits and Pulse Surveys, helping organizations implement equitable practices. Her work has made an impact with clients like The City of Berkeley, Sherwin Williams, and Sempra. She also delivers powerful workshops at top educational institutions, reflecting her commitment to organizational effectiveness.

With a background in Psychology and Business Management, Tiana is a sought-after speaker, contributing author, and a passionate advocate for sustainable leadership development.

Inclusive Leadership

By Dr. Nicole Yeldell Butts

Executives are pivotal in the creation of organizational culture. The new C-suite leader will need to be intentional and purposeful about the organizational culture they wish to create and how they go about creating it. Without this intentionality, culture will be organic, and haphazard, without deliberate planning or conscious effort by leadership to define or shape it.

Contemporary workplaces tend to be diverse in population, but this diversity does not inevitably give rise to inclusive organizational cultures. Inclusive organizational cultures are a result of intentional efforts to foster respect, equity, and belonging among every employee. It involves creating environments where all employees feel valued, heard, and empowered to contribute their perspectives and ideas. Inclusive organizational cultures are not created haphazardly, rather, they stem from deliberate strategies to cultivate specific values, norms, and behaviors, and an ongoing, unwavering commitment from leadership.

This chapter will focus on the importance and creation of an inclusive organizational culture, through the encouragement, enablement, and valuing of employee ideas.

The 1955 murder of Emmett Till, a fourteen-year-old African American boy, shocked the world and propelled the U.S. Civil Rights Movement. Sixty-five years later, the murder of George Floyd sparked civil protest, calls for racial reckoning, and demands for justice and equity. Many organizations responded to the national outcry for justice by releasing public statements supporting diversity and anti-racism, pledging solidarity and committing to racial equity. Yet nearly six decades after the Civil Rights Act of 1964 was signed, American society as a whole and companies, specifically, still struggle to actualize diversity, equity, and inclusion (DEI).

As I write this in 2024, organizational DEI is not a new concept. It has existed in a variety of forms under numerous names for decades, evolving from diversity awareness or sensitivity to the growth and addition of inclusion, equity, belonging, access, and accountability. But the pendulum is always in motion, and as Tiana talked about in a previous chapter, the past year has seen a significant devolution of DEI in which it has become the monster under America's bed, being blamed for everything from making children feel uncomfortable, to a bridge collapse in Baltimore.

As a DEI practitioner for more than 20 years, I have experienced this evolution and devolution. In my professional capacity, I have seen firsthand the impact that executives have on the success or failure of their organizational DEI efforts. I have encountered executives who silently resist, and those who silently support DEI. I have seen those who explicitly resist, those who explicitly support, and those who appear simply perplexed and noncommittal.

The executives I have worked most successfully with are those who genuinely support the intention, concept and value of DEI, yet have been unsure how to go about it. It is for these executives and the organizations they lead that I wanted to write this chapter focussing on a singular and highly achievable aspect of DEI.

Many organizations have been successful in creating a diverse workforce but far fewer have been successful in creating an inclusive organizational culture. Let's be clear – simply having diversity does not equate with inclusion. Creating a diverse workforce and fostering an inclusive workplace are two very different endeavors. You may even notice that as you work to diversify your workforce, the turnover of diverse staff increases. Just as hiring requires specific efforts, so too does retention.

A critical skill of the new C-suite leader is the ability to create an inclusive organizational culture that embraces diverse perspectives, fosters innovation, enhances employee engagement, and better serves customers and communities. Creating an inclusive culture requires that leaders ensure diverse perspectives, experiences, and talents are encouraged, enabled, and valued. Valuing everyone's ideas is critical to building a positive and inclusive organizational culture, and signals that the organization is committed to diversity, equity, and inclusion.

One of my clients, Johnathan, a CEO of a tech company prided himself on fostering an environment of innovation. A few setbacks, including projects becoming increasingly similar, and lacking the creativity that once set the company apart, caused him to ponder his self-assessment. One afternoon, during a routine check-in with department heads, Johnathan noticed a pattern emerging: the same voices dominated discussions, while others remained conspicuously silent. Concerned, he decided to delve deeper into understanding the dynamics at play. He scheduled a series of one-on-one meetings with team members, and in these candid conversations he learned firsthand about the hesitations and barriers that prevented some team members from sharing their ideas openly. One person shared how she often felt her suggestions were overlooked or dismissed in favor of more vocal colleagues. Another expressed feeling unsure about cultural norms in meetings. Still, another mentioned not wanting to appear contrary to the direction of the larger group.

Organizational culture significantly impacts how ideas are shared and valued. The intention of the new C-suite leader should be to foster an organizational culture that actively, intentionally, and purposefully encourages, enables, and values input from all employees at every level. Pixar Animation Studios, the maker of films including Toy Story, Up, and Finding Nemo, has the credo "ideas can come from anywhere" which fosters a culture where everyone is encouraged to speak up.

Creating an organizational culture in which all employees are encouraged and empowered to have a voice, and then knowing that their unique voice is valued is critical to the creation of an inclusive culture. This is not simply a DEI program or initiative, but rather an intentional creation of culture.

Psychological Safety and the Reciprocal Nature of Ideas and Inclusion

The relationship between encouraging, enabling, and valuing employee's ideas and an inclusive organizational culture is mutually reinforcing and reciprocal. When an inclusive environment is cultivated, it encourages the generation and sharing of diverse ideas. Conversely, encouraging and valuing diverse ideas fosters a sense of inclusion among employees. Embracing diverse ideas broadens the perspectives within an organization and enhances inclusion. This inclusivity in thought fosters a culture of respect and value for different viewpoints.

Critical to this relationship is psychological safety. Psychological safety impacts people's perceptions of the consequences of taking interpersonal risks. Organizational research has identified psychological safety as a critical factor in understanding workplace behaviors, highlighting that it facilitates the willing contribution of activities such as sharing information and knowledge, speaking up with suggestions for organizational improvements, and taking initiative to develop new products and services.

As you read about in the chapter, Visionary Leadership, Amy Edmondson, Professor of Leadership at Harvard Business School, and author of seven books, including The Fearless Organization: Creating Psychological Safety in the Workplace for Learning, Innovation, and Growth, found that psychological safety is essential for fostering a climate where individuals feel comfortable sharing their ideas and taking interpersonal risks. Reciprocally, an inclusive environment creates psychological safety, in which employees feel secure to express their thoughts and ideas without fear of ridicule or negative consequences. This safety is critical for encouraging participation. Without it, people withhold ideas. Edmondson refers to it as an epidemic of silence.

In my role as a C-suite leader, I employ four primary strategies to foster psychological safety and prevent the epidemic of silence - vulnerability, conversations, failure, and synergy.

I practice personal vulnerability, believing it is a powerful agent for building deeper, more meaningful connections and fostering an environment where others feel safe to express themselves without fear of negative consequences. I demonstrate vulnerability by sharing my authentic self, rather than putting up a façade to appear strong or perfect. I am transparent about my experiences, limitations, setbacks, failures, and uncertainties. I openly ask for help, seeking input and assistance from team members, acknowledging that I don't have all the answers. Most importantly, I actively solicit, act on, and follow up on personal feedback.

Teams I work with come to expect that I will ask them for critical feedback, receive it openly, act on it as appropriate, and follow up on the outcomes based on their feedback. This practice not only helps me become a better leader for individuals and the team but also demonstrates that I value their perspectives, recognize my imperfections, and am committed to personal growth for the benefit of myself, the team, and the organization.

Initiate and engage in difficult conversations. Regularly addressing tough topics can improve overall communication within the team, making it easier to discuss issues openly and honestly, and showing team members that their concerns are taken seriously. When leaders handle difficult conversations with vulnerability, respect, and empathy it reinforces a culture where team members feel valued and respected. This approach encourages others to initiate and participate in difficult conversations, which builds both individual and collective skills in managing such discussions effectively.

Normalize and welcome failure. Failure is a natural part of any journey. Leaders must demonstrate that making mistakes is not only okay but vital to learning, creativity, and innovation. Welcoming failure is crucial for fostering psychological safety, as it creates an environment where team members feel safe to take risks, innovate, and learn from their experiences. I normalize failure by sharing my own mistakes and the lessons I've learned, celebrating effort and learning regardless of the outcome, and encouraging realistic project timelines that allow time for mistakes, lessons learned and refinements.

In one organization where risk-taking, mistakes, and failures were treated particularly harshly, I sought to change this cultural norm, normalize failure, and encourage a growth mindset. To achieve this, I implemented an online "failure wall" where all employees, especially leaders, were encouraged to post about mistakes they made and what they learned from them. Initially, the participation was limited to minor mistakes, but as employees observed supportive and constructive comments from leaders and peers, they became increasingly transparent and started sharing significant mistakes. After a year, we noticed a remarkable shift: employees were openly discussing mistakes in meetings and actively seeking input.

Promote and advocate for synergy, asserting that our collective and cooperative efforts will produce a greater impact than what could be accomplished independently. When we work effectively in collaboration, building on and refining ideas together, we achieve results that exceed what any one of us could have achieved individually. When ideas are raised, we work collectively to explore and refine them rather than dismissing them outright or making them the sole responsibility of the person who proposed them. By promoting and advocating for synergy, an expectation is created that we develop ideas cooperatively, collaboratively, and collectively, drawing on the diverse skill sets, thought processes, experiences, and perspectives of the team.

The relationship between ideas and inclusion is symbiotic. Inclusion fosters a climate where diverse ideas are freely shared, leading to greater innovation and creativity. In turn, the active valuing of diverse ideas enhances the sense of inclusion among employees, driving engagement and better organizational outcomes. The new C-suite leaders who prioritize psychological safety create a dynamic, and inclusive work environment.

Organizational Impact of Valuing Employees' Ideas

A 2017 Gallup report indicates that inclusive cultures lead to higher employee engagement, which in turn drives continuous idea generation and organizational improvement. Inclusion fosters an environment encouraging continuous improvement. Employees are more likely to suggest improvements and innovations when they feel their input is valued.

My client Johnathan realized that by not actively encouraging diverse perspectives, he was missing out on a wealth of untapped potential, innovative solutions, and creative approaches. He learned that fostering an environment where diverse perspectives are encouraged and valued leads to numerous organizational benefits.

Let's examine some of these organizational benefits including enhanced creativity and innovation, improved decision-making, expansion of your customer base, greater internal equity and fairness, stronger team dynamics, and greater employee engagement.

Enhanced Creativity and Innovation

Inclusive environments encouraging diverse ideas tend to be more innovative. Different perspectives and experiences lead to unique viewpoints and ideas that broaden the range of possible solutions and encourage out-of-the-box thinking. A 2017 PriceWaterhouseCoopers' Innovation Benchmark Report found that the companies identified as top innovators achieve, on average, 5.6% higher profit margins.

I experienced this phenomenon directly with an executive

leadership team in a professional services firm, where as a result of enhanced creativity and innovation, their organization saw a 20% increase in sales and a 15% reduction in material costs, significantly boosting the company's profit margins. Such outcomes may not emerge in organizational cultures that lack psychological safety.

Improved Decision-Making and Decision Quality

Diverse ideas contribute to better decision-making processes. A diverse set of ideas allows for a comprehensive understanding of problems and challenges. When a range of perspectives is considered, decisions are more likely to be well-rounded and effective. his variety of viewpoints, approaches, and solutions encourages critical thinking, leading to effective, comprehensive problem-solving and thorough analysis, which ultimately improves decision-making processes. Diverse perspectives also reduce the risk of groupthink.

Olivia, one of my coaching clients focused on building her inclusive leadership skills, found that by leveraging diverse perspectives within her organization, a newly formed team was able to identify potential challenges and opportunities that had been overlooked by a previous, more homogeneous team. These newly identified challenges and opportunities provided Olivia and the team with enhanced strategic insights and decision-making capabilities.

Understanding and Serving a Diverse Customer Base

Organizations that value diverse ideas are better placed to understand and meet the needs of a diverse customer base and position their organizations for greater success and sustainability in a competitive market. Inclusivity in idea generation ensures that products and services are designed with a broader range of users in mind, enhancing customer satisfaction and loyalty. This leads to effective marketing strategies and products that appeal to a wider audience.

I saw the impact of this firsthand while working with an executive leadership team in the technology industry. By intentionally embracing diverse ideas in their product development process, they were able to enhance their understanding of various customer needs, resulting in the launch of inclusive software solutions catering to a diverse user base. This approach not only boosted customer satisfaction and loyalty but also strengthened the company's market presence, allowing it to effectively compete and thrive in a competitive industry landscape, which resulted in increased sales and brand recognition.

Equity & Fairness

An inclusive environment where everyone's ideas are considered reduces feelings of marginalization among underrepresented groups. Encouraging input from all individuals helps mitigate biases and prevents dominant voices from overshadowing others. This ensures a fairer process where decisions are made based on the best ideas rather than the loudest or most powerful voices.

My client Johnathan saw the impact of his efforts to encourage, enable, and value employee ideas with a focus on inclusivity of diverse perspectives, in the bi-annual employee survey results. The survey highlighted significant improvements in workplace inclusivity, with over 85% of respondents reporting that they feel more valued and respected for their contributions. Additionally, there was a notable decrease in instances where ideas from underrepresented groups and employees in non-leadership positions felt marginalized. The survey revealed a strong consensus that decision-making processes had become fairer, emphasizing participation over hierarchy.

Strengthen Team Dynamics

When team members know that their ideas are valued, it fosters a culture of trust and collaboration. People are more willing to share their thoughts and support each other, leading to stronger team cohesion. Psychological safety, which is crucial for team dynamics, is enhanced when everyone feels that their contributions matter.

An employee survey from one of my client companies indicated a notable increase in team cohesion, satisfaction, and innovation following efforts to foster inclusivity. The survey revealed that over 75% of employees reported a greater sense of trust and camaraderie among team members, attributing this to improved communication and mutual support.

Greater Employee Engagement

According to a 2020 Catalyst report, workplaces where diverse ideas are welcomed see higher levels of employee engagement and innovation. Employees who feel that their perspectives are valued are engaged and committed to their work. This sense of inclusion leads to higher job satisfaction and lower turnover rates. Gallup research indicates that employee engagement is strongly linked to positive business outcomes, including lower absenteeism and turnover, as well as higher productivity and profitability. When employees see their ideas being implemented, it empowers them and reinforces their sense of belonging. This empowerment leads to higher engagement and loyalty to the organization. A study by Deloitte shows that organizations with inclusive cultures are more likely to be innovative and agile, as employees feel more connected and committed.

Employee surveys continue to be a great measure of success, even when they only reveal an increase in participation. The average response rate for employee surveys is typically between 30%-50% with some high-performing organizations seeing participation rates of 60%-70%. One of my clients historically had participation rates of

45%-55%. Once they began encouraging, enabling, and valuing employee ideas, their survey response rates skyrocketed to 75%. This is a remarkable indicator for employee engagement because when employees feel engaged, they are more inclined to be involved in initiatives that affect the workplace, including surveys. Increased survey response rates can indicate that employees believe their voices matter, the organization values their input, and they trust the organization to act on their feedback. A culture that promotes feedback and values employee opinions tends to have higher survey response rates. This culture of inclusivity and participation is both a result and a driver of higher employee engagement.

Valuing Employees' Ideas Sends a Powerful Message

When employees know their ideas matter, it communicates a powerful message of value, trust, inclusion, and respect. This can lead to higher levels of engagement, satisfaction, and loyalty, as employees feel more connected to the organization and motivated to contribute their best. Ultimately, it creates a positive and dynamic workplace culture where everyone feels empowered to share their insights and drive the organization forward.

When employees see that their ideas matter, it sends several powerful and positive messages that significantly impact motivation, engagement, and overall perception of the organization.

As an executive coach and consultant, I often talk with employees of my coaching clients. It is through these conversations that I hear, understand, and can share the message employees receive when their ideas are encouraged, enabled, and valued

You Are Valued

Employees feel that their contributions are recognized and appreciated. This recognition reinforces their sense of value within the organization. It communicates that their unique perspectives and skills are important to the company's success. By valuing employees' ideas, the organization demonstrates a commitment to their professional growth, and shows that the company sees them as capable of contributing valuable insights and solutions. This leads to increasing opportunities for employees to develop their skills, take on new challenges, and advance in their careers.

Emily, an employee working for one of my clients expressed her sense of being valued by saying, "Since the company started focusing on creating an inclusive work culture, I feel that my contributions are genuinely recognized and appreciated. Knowing that my unique perspectives and skills are important to our success makes me feel truly valued. This commitment to welcoming our ideas shows me that they see me as a capable contributor."

Your Voice Matters

It signals that the organization values open communication, and every employee has a voice. This empowers employees to speak up, share ideas, and contribute to discussions. Employees feel that their opinions and insights are heard and considered, which boosts their confidence and willingness to participate. Ed Catmull, the former President of Pixar, understands this as he writes in his book, Creativity, Inc., "A movie is not one idea, it's a multitude of them. And behind these ideas are people."

Marcus, an employee who had worked at one of my client's companies for less than a year shared, "Since being here, I've felt empowered to speak up and share my ideas. It's clear that open communication is valued here, and then knowing that my opinions and insights are heard and considered has really boosted my confidence and willingness to participate. And when I think about some of our projects, I can see the diverse voices and ideas of our team behind them."

You Belong Here

When ideas from all employees are sought and valued, it fosters a sense of belonging. Employees feel included and integral to the team. This inclusivity helps to build a supportive and collaborative workplace culture where everyone feels they have a place and leads to higher levels of engagement and job satisfaction. Employees who feel heard are more likely to be motivated and committed to their work, leading to lower turnover rates and higher productivity.

Jasmine shared, "Since the company started actively seeking ideas from all employees, I truly feel like I belong here. Being included and knowing that my contributions are integral to the team has made me feel more connected and supported. This is a place I can see myself being at for a long time."

We Trust You

Valuing employees' ideas demonstrates trust in their judgment and capabilities. It shows the organization respects their knowledge and expertise. Trusting employees to contribute ideas leads to increased autonomy and responsibility, enhancing job satisfaction.

One client's employee, Kevin, expressed his sense of organizational trust by saying, "I feel that my leadership team genuinely trusts my judgment and capabilities because they consistently value ideas coming from me and our team. This respect for my knowledge and expertise has given me a greater sense of autonomy and responsibility. Knowing that the leadership team believes in my contributions makes me feel empowered and motivated to excel."

We Are Open to Change and Innovation

An organization that values employees' ideas shows that it is open to change and innovation. It indicates a willingness to listen and adapt based on input from all levels. This message has the ability to inspire a culture of continuous improvement and creativity, encouraging employees to think critically and innovatively.

Sarah shared, "What I most appreciate about this company is that it is always open to new ideas. I have been at companies that don't want to change. They just go with the status quo. This company is willing to listen and adapt based on input from all levels of employees. Continuous improvement and creativity are not just words here. They are real. It encourages me to think critically and come up with innovative solutions, knowing that my contributions can drive positive change."

We Are All in This Together

It reinforces the idea that the organization is a collaborative environment where everyone's input is crucial to success. It promotes teamwork and the idea that all employees are working towards common goals. This message fosters a sense of unity and collective effort, enhancing team cohesion and morale.

David, a long-term employee of one of my clients shared "I notice how Monica continually reinforces the idea that we're a collaborative team where everyone's input matters. It really promotes teamwork and the understanding that each of us plays a crucial role in achieving our common goals. This message of unity fosters a strong sense of camaraderie and collective effort, which boosts our team cohesion and morale, making me proud to be part of her team and this company."

Valuing All Ideas Does Not Mean Implementing All Ideas

Encouraging and valuing everyone's ideas does not necessarily mean implementing every idea. Instead, it means ensuring that all employees feel their ideas are heard, considered, and valued. These are distinct concepts that play different roles in fostering a healthy and innovative organizational culture. Valuing all ideas means recognizing, appreciating, and considering every idea shared by employees, regardless of whether these ideas are ultimately implemented. It involves creating an environment where all contributions are respected and seen as valuable to the collective brainstorming and decision-making process. Implementing all ideas means taking action on every idea that is proposed by employees, and putting them into practice regardless of feasibility, alignment with strategic goals, or resource constraints.

Valuing all ideas doesn't mean implementing every idea. It's about fostering an inclusive and supportive environment where every contribution is respected and considered. It focuses on building a culture of openness and psychological safety, encouraging continuous idea generation. Implementing all ideas on the other hand, is neither practical nor beneficial due to resource constraints, strategic misalignment, and the need for thorough evaluation of each idea's feasibility and potential impact. The key is to value all ideas by acknowledging and considering them, while selectively implementing those that align with organizational goals, and at the same time are feasible, and promise substantial benefits. This approach balances inclusivity with practical decision-making, leading to sustainable innovation and growth.

Common Barriers to Valuing Employees Ideas

Reflecting on my client Johnathan, he came to realize that simply understanding the importance of diverse ideas was not enough. Fostering a culture that truly embraced these perspectives required identifying and dismantling the barriers that prevented them. As we studied the culture within the organization, we became acutely aware of both the overt and subtle barriers that hindered the inclusion of diverse perspectives, spanning from organizational culture to individual biases. Barriers ranged from unconscious biases that favored familiar ideas to systemic issues that inadvertently silenced some voices. One prominent barrier was the company's existing meeting structure. Traditional meetings often allowed the most vocal participants to dominate, unintentionally sidelining quieter team members.

Johnathan realized these barriers were perpetuated by unintentional biases—managers often gravitated towards familiar ideas, and there was a lack of structured opportunities for all voices to be heard. Even well-meaning managers tended to favor ideas from individuals who thought and communicated similarly to them. This bias often excludes innovative concepts from employees with different backgrounds, experiences, or communication styles.

Including employees' ideas in the organizational decision-making process can be challenging due to several common barriers, some of which Johnathan found. These barriers often inhibit open communication, reduce employee engagement, and ultimately stifle innovation. Let's explore some of the most common barriers:

Fear of Negative Consequences

Within organizations that lack psychological safety, employees may fear ridicule, retribution, or negative consequences for sharing their ideas, particularly those that do not align with the status quo. This fear leads to reluctance to voice their thoughts – the epidemic of silence.

Cultural Norms and Rigid Hierarchies

Organizational culture significantly impacts how ideas are shared and valued. In some organizational cultures, there may be an implicit understanding that only certain individuals or departments are responsible for generating ideas. This marginalizes others and limits diverse contributions. In organizations with rigid hierarchical structures, lower-level employees may feel that their ideas are less valued or that they do not have the authority to contribute to decision-making.

Mistrust in Leadership

According to a 2014 study by the American Psychological Association, trust in leadership is a key factor in whether employees feel comfortable sharing ideas. If employees do not trust their leaders or believe that their ideas will not be taken seriously, they are less likely to share their thoughts.

Poor Communication Channels and Inadequate Feedback Loops

Ineffective communication channels hinder the flow of ideas. Employees need clear and accessible ways to share their suggestions. The International Journal of Business Communication emphasizes the importance of effective communication channels for facilitating idea-sharing in organizations. Without proper feedback mechanisms, employees might feel that their ideas are ignored or unappreciated. This lack of feedback can discourage future contributions. Effective feedback systems are essential for maintaining employee engagement in the idea-generation process.

Status Quo

Employees and leaders alike may resist change due to comfort with the status quo or fear of the unknown. This resistance prevents the consideration and implementation of new ideas. Such unique solutions and approaches may not emerge in organizational cultures that rely on rigid hierarchies and have become accustomed to the status quo of silence or in which psychological safety does not exist.

Implicit Bias

Bias is a barrier to inclusion, and hinders our ability to create psychological safety, which we know is necessary to build creative, collaborative, and high-performing teams. Implicit bias significantly impacts decision-making processes and the inclusion of diverse ideas. Implicit biases lead to certain ideas being valued over others based on the identity of the person presenting them. This stifles diverse perspectives and contributions.

Addressing these common organizational barriers creates an environment in which all employees feel empowered to share their ideas, leading to greater innovation and organizational success. To effectively include employees' ideas, organizations must address these barriers by fostering a culture of psychological safety, trust, and transparency; providing effective feedback mechanisms; ensuring clear communication channels; and actively working to overcome resistance to change and biases.

How New C-suite Leaders Ensure Everyone's Ideas Matter

My client Johnathan acknowledged that inclusive leadership required dismantling these barriers and implementing policies and practices that actively ensured every voice, regardless of rank or role, felt valued and empowered. Armed with newfound insights and determined to transform the organizational culture, Johnathan embarked on a mission to foster an environment where diverse ideas and perspectives were not only encouraged but celebrated.

The approach we developed was multifaceted. Johnathan implemented structured initiatives to encourage and amplify diverse voices. He introduced rotating facilitators for meetings to ensure all team members had an opportunity to lead discussions. He instituted a "no interruption" policy during brainstorming sessions, where every idea, regardless of origin, was given equal consideration. He chose to lead by example, actively seeking out and championing diverse voices within the company. Johnathan publicly acknowledged and celebrated contributions from team members, reinforcing the message that the company thrived not just on grand visions but on the collective wisdom and creativity of every team member.

Over time, Johnathan witnessed a transformation. Meetings buzzed with energy and inclusivity, and innovative ideas flowed from all corners of the company. Products developed with diverse input became more robust and well-received in the market, reflecting the varied perspectives that shaped them. The barriers that once hindered inclusivity gradually crumbled, replaced by a culture where every employee felt valued, respected, and empowered to contribute their best ideas.

Allow me a moment to pause and be abundantly clear about something. I have been extremely intentional about using the language "encourage, enable, and value." What I may not have made clear is that these words are neither synonymous nor interchangeable. Each word represents a unique focus and intention and requires its own unique strategies. Leaders can encourage but not enable. Leaders can enable something but not value it. I have seen leaders do one of these things without the others and not achieve the desired results.

Think of it this way: Encouraging employees to share their ideas is akin to inviting them to provide input or pose challenging questions. I can ask for their input, but without enabling the right conditions for them to do so, their engagement is unlikely. Enabling involves establishing norms and systems that facilitate input, as well as removing any barriers that hinder participation. If these systems are not in place or barriers persist, I am not effectively enabling employees to provide the input I seek. Encouragement and enablement are necessary, however, without valuing input, employees will likely cease to share. Valuing input entails considering it seriously, engaging with it, providing feedback, and potentially implementing the ideas. These three elements form a triangle, and without any one of the elements, the structure becomes unstable and incomplete.

The new C-suite leader is responsible for building and maintaining this triangle. To support you in doing so, below are several strategies to encourage, enable, and value input.

Develop an Organizational Value for Employee Input

Recall Pixar's credo, "Ideas can come from anywhere," fostering a culture in which everyone is encouraged to speak up. Cleary articulate the importance of employee input as a core organizational value. For example, "We believe that every team member's perspective is crucial to our success. We are committed to listening to and valuing the contributions of all employees."

Model Inclusive Behavior

Lead by example. Demonstrate inclusive behavior by actively asking for input, listening to, and engaging with employee ideas. Show genuine interest and curiosity about contributions. Ensure that all voices are heard during discussions, especially those who may be less vocal or from underrepresented groups. For many years across multiple positions, I had a meme posted prominently in my office that read, "The next time you are afraid to share an idea, remember someone once said, 'Let's make a movie about a tornado full of sharks.'" If you don't get this reference, I invite you to look up Sharknado which at this point in 2024 has six Sharknado films and a video game. People must feel safe and welcome to offer different ideas; it is your responsibility to model this behavior.

Ensure Psychological Safety

Foster a psychologically safe environment where employees feel safe sharing unconventional ideas and feel comfortable taking risks without fear of negative consequences. Address and mitigate any behaviors or practices that have the potential to intimidate or silence employees, ensuring a respectful and supportive atmosphere. Remember, my four tips for creating psychological safety are to share personal vulnerability, engage in difficult conversations, welcome failure, and advocate for synergy. Encourage collaborative refinement of ideas. Sometimes an initial idea may need further development or adjustments to be viable. Facilitate discussions and workshops where ideas can be improved upon collectively. Create teams or task forces to explore and refine promising ideas.

Create Structured Opportunities for Input and Evaluate Ideas Fairly

Hold regular brainstorming sessions and innovation meetings in which employees can share ideas on various topics or projects. Ensure these sessions are structured, allowing equal participation.

Use techniques such as round-robin or silent brainstorming to give everyone an opportunity to contribute. Provide various platforms for employees to share ideas, such as suggestion boxes, team meetings, brainstorming sessions, and digital collaboration tools. Make it clear that all ideas are welcome and will be given due consideration.

Develop clear criteria for evaluating ideas based on factors such as feasibility, alignment with organizational goals, potential impact, and resource requirements. In order for employees to understand how decisions are made, ensure that the evaluation process is transparent and consistent.

Allocate Time

Time is a critical element in the process of encouraging and valuing ideas. Time is needed for people to think creatively and generate ideas. Project management plans need to incorporate and allocate time for structured opportunities for input, review, refinement, and feedback. You cannot expect synergy or welcome failure if you do not allow the time needed.

Recognize and Celebrate Contributions

Acknowledge all contributions, give feedback, and show appreciation for the effort put into generating ideas. Recognize and celebrate the effort of employees who contribute ideas, and collaborate on refining ideas, regardless of whether their suggestions are implemented. Utilize formal and informal recognition systems to highlight contributions. This could be through verbal acknowledgments, awards, shout-outs in meetings, and highlighting contributions in company communications. Create a culture of appreciation where employees feel their efforts to contribute are seen and valued. Clearly communicate that not all projects or ideas will succeed, however, it's the learning process that's most valuable.

Enact Feedback Loops

Inclusive environments provide regular feedback on ideas, which help employees grow and refine their thinking. By implementing a structured feedback loop, organizations cultivate an environment where the sharing of ideas is nurtured, valued, and continually improved upon, fostering innovation and achieving sustainable growth. It's important to provide constructive feedback on why certain ideas may not be pursued and to maintain transparency about the decision-making process related to idea evaluation. Creating a system for tracking and acting on suggestions is essential. Regularly update employees on the status of their ideas, regardless of whether they are being implemented, further evaluated, or deemed not feasible. When an idea cannot be pursued, offer constructive feedback and reasoning. Discuss current priorities, resource constraints, or strategic direction, ensuring employees understand their input is still valued.

Conclusion

As Johnathan reflected on his journey, he realized that fostering a culture of inclusive ideas wasn't just about business success—it was about creating a workplace where individuals knew that their voices mattered, and their contributions made a difference. As the company continued to grow and innovate, Johnathan knew that embracing diversity and inclusion wasn't just the right thing to do— it was the key to unlocking limitless potential and shaping a brighter future for the company and employees alike.

By implementing these strategies, the new C-suite leader creates an environment where all employees feel their ideas matter. This leads to greater engagement, innovation, and overall organizational success. Leaders who prioritize inclusivity and value diverse perspectives foster a culture of respect and collaboration, empowering everyone to contribute their best ideas. Doing so involves listening to, evaluating, and providing feedback on ideas, not necessarily implementing every single one. By managing this process effectively, leaders foster a culture of innovation, respect, and continuous improvement, ensuring that employees remain engaged and motivated to contribute their best ideas

As the pendulum on DEI invariably swings, and American society's views on DEI ebb and flow, the ability to create organizational cultures that encourage, enable, and value employee ideas will benefit the new C-suite leader, marginalized groups in the workplace, and aid American society in becoming more just and equitable.

About Dr. Nicole L. Yeldell Butts

CEO, NLYB Solutions

Meet Dr. Nicole L. Yeldell Butts, a dynamic C-suite executive, executive coach, and sought-after public speaker with a 25-year career dedicated to organizational transformation.

As the CEO of NLYB Solutions, Nicole guides executives and leadership teams through personal and organizational change with her proven five-step framework, SHIFT, which has driven measurable and sustainable transformation across numerous organizations.

Nicole's academic credentials include a doctorate in Organizational Change & Leadership from the University of Southern California, complemented by degrees from Howard University and Bowie State University.

Nicole is also a certified mediator with multiple professional certifications.

Beyond her professional achievements, Nicole is deeply committed to philanthropy, with notable volunteer work including her service at the United Nations World Conference Against Racism. When she's not leading change, Nicole enjoys international travel, jazz festivals, and spending time with her beloved dogs.

Ethical Leadership

By Andy Fee

Businesses today are finding it harder and harder. The world's more connected than ever, and rapid change is the only constant. Organizations face increasing pressure to innovate and stay ahead of the competition while also upholding high ethical standards. The New C-suite demands a breed of leaders who possess a multifaceted skill set. These executives must be contemplative, carefully considering the implications of their decisions and actions. They should exhibit a sharp intellect, enabling them to navigate complex challenges and devise smart solutions. Innovation is crucial, as leaders must be able to think creatively and drive their organizations forward in a rapidly evolving world.

Resilience is essential, allowing leaders to bounce back from setbacks and adapt to changing circumstances. However, above all else, the most critical attribute for today's C-suite leaders is a strong ethical foundation. Integrity, honesty, and a commitment to doing what is right must be the guiding principles that inform every decision and action taken by those at the helm of an organization.

The pursuit of innovation should not come at the expense of integrity. Ethical leadership plays a crucial role in fostering a culture of innovation while ensuring that the organization operates responsibly. This chapter explores the vital importance of ethics in modern business, the link between ethical leadership and innovation, and guidance for building and maintaining a thriving culture of integrity.

Why Should You Care?

I have spent over a quarter century in the college athletics industry, culminating in my tenure at Long Beach State University as the Director of Athletics. What I learned over this time is that leadership in college athletics demands a delicate balance between competitive success and the holistic development of student-athletes. Over the years, I've learned that ethical leadership is the cornerstone of this balance. It involves making decisions that prioritize integrity, fairness, and the well-being of all stakeholders. It's about setting a standard that others can look up to, ensuring our actions consistently reflect our values.

One of the key lessons I've learned is the importance of transparency and accountability. In a field where the pressure to succeed can be immense, it's crucial to maintain open lines of communication and to be accountable for our actions and decisions. These builds trust and respect, not just within our teams, but also with the broader community.

In essence, my years in college athletics have taught me that ethical leadership is about more than just leading teams to victory. It's about shaping a culture that prioritizes integrity, inclusivity, and the overall development of student-athletes, ensuring that we leave a positive, lasting impact on both individuals and the broader community.

The Human Element

Beyond the business case, ethics is fundamentally about people. Every decision ultimately impacts human beings, whether they be employees, customers, suppliers, communities or shareholders. Ethical lapses often stem from losing sight of this human element amid daily business pressures. The 1984 Union Carbide gas leak that killed thousands resulted from multiple ignored employee safety warnings. In the early 2000s, pharmaceutical companies fueled the devastating opioid epidemic by unethically downplaying addiction risks.

Great leaders never forget that their choices affect real people's lives. During my five years leading the Long Beach State University Athletics Department, our credo was to provide the best possible experience for our student-athletes, both in the classroom and on the field.

About two months into my tenure, the track and field head coach informed me that one of his athletes, who was about to head to the NCAA Nationals Meet, had been caught forging a doctor's note. We discussed the athlete and the circumstances surrounding the issue. Making it to the NCAA Nationals Meet is extremely difficult, and the results affect team scores and qualifying marks. We faced a tough decision: suspend the athlete immediately, forfeiting potential points and a good finish at the NCAA National Meet, or let them compete with a suspension the following season. Ultimately, we chose to suspend the athlete immediately. This decision not only impacted the athlete who forged the note but also their teammates who were counting on them to contribute to the team's success. It wasn't the decision I had hoped to make so early in my role, but ethical leaders must make difficult, sometimes gut-wrenching decisions that can have a ripple effect.

Pausing to consider the people involved can bring moral clarity to tough business decisions. Who could be helped or harmed? Are we treating all with empathy and fairness? Is this a choice we would feel good explaining to our loved ones? As a leader in the NCAA Collegiate Athletics field, I remind myself that ethical conduct comes more naturally when I remember there are real people on the receiving end.

The Foundations of Ethical Leadership

Ethical leadership is rooted in integrity, fairness, respect for others, and alignment between words and actions. Even under pressure, ethical leaders make decisions based on strong moral principles rather than just short-term interests. By consistently modeling these values, they build trust with stakeholders and inspire everyone to operate with integrity, creating a positive ripple effect throughout the organization. Upon assuming the role of Director of Athletics at Long Beach State University in 2017, I recognized the importance of leading by example. If I expected ethical conduct from others, I had to embody those principles myself, setting a visible standard for everyone to follow.

Trust is the foundation upon which innovation thrives. Ethical leadership fosters a culture of psychological safety, transparent communication, and room for experimentation—the essential ingredients for innovative thinking. Ethical leaders strike a balance between encouraging responsible risk-taking and idea-sharing, while maintaining clear guidelines for conduct. They actively promote collaboration among stakeholders to ensure innovations benefit everyone and encourage open dialogue to address potential issues early on.

An ethical framework prevents innovation becoming irresponsible. At Long Beach State University, we operated under a deontological framework, emphasizing moral duties and rules, where actions are inherently right or wrong, regardless of consequences. The principle "Always Do the Right Thing" was consistently emphasized during my tenure as Athletics Director. While "doing the right thing" can be challenging, success is achieved when this framework is effectively communicated to staff, who then integrate it into their daily lives. Coaches and staff would often respond with a smile and the phrase "Doing the right thing to make a difference!" when asked about their impact on the student-athlete experience.

Building and Sustaining an Ethical Culture of Innovation

Ultimately, an organization's ethical conduct is a direct reflection of the daily actions and decisions made by its members, from the top leadership down to the frontline staff. Leaders, however, play a particularly crucial role in shaping this conduct. They set the tone for the entire organization, establishing and reinforcing the values and standards that guide ethical behavior.

Leaders embed integrity into an organization through a multifaceted approach:

Setting a clear ethical vision: Leaders must articulate a compelling vision for ethical conduct that aligns with the organization's mission and values. This vision should be communicated clearly and consistently throughout the organization, providing a shared understanding of what ethical behavior looks like in practice. As a leader, I have constantly communicated what behaviors we wanted and celebrated employees that demonstrated those behaviors as examples of our goal.

Establishing and enforcing ethical standards: Leaders must develop and implement clear and comprehensive ethical standards and codes of conduct. These standards should cover all aspects of the organization's operations and be regularly reviewed and updated to ensure their relevance.

Modeling ethical behavior: Leaders must lead by example, consistently demonstrating integrity and ethical conduct in their own actions and decisions. This sets a powerful precedent for others to follow and reinforces the importance of ethical behavior within the organization.

Creating a culture of integrity: Leaders must foster a culture where ethical behavior is valued, encouraged, and rewarded. This involves creating safe spaces for open communication, empowering employees to raise ethical concerns, and celebrating those who uphold ethical standards.

Providing ethical training and resources: Leaders must ensure that employees have the necessary training and resources to understand and apply ethical principles in their work. This includes providing regular ethics training, offering guidance on ethical dilemmas, and creating channels for reporting ethical violations.

Thorough education within your organization is crucial for successfully implementing the ethical leadership concepts discussed above. At Long Beach State University, I brought in a highly skilled educator and consultant to help my leadership team onboard coaches and staff for the department's upcoming initiatives. This investment in education and training ensures that ethical conduct becomes ingrained in the organization's very fabric, transforming it from a mere aspiration into a lived reality. This not only safeguards the organization's reputation and minimizes risks but also nurtures trust, engagement, and loyalty among employees and stakeholders. Let your organization know loud and clear that ethics will lead decision making with their best interests at heart.

These practices make ethics a habitual part of company life, equipping people to navigate complex moral quandaries. By proactively building a culture that prizes doing the right thing, organizations prevent ethical crises rather than just reacting to them. My goal as the department's leader was to ensure that focusing on doing what's right would snowball into decisions that, in the long run, bore more fruit than taking shortcuts or sidesteps.

The Link Between Ethics and Innovation

Innovation thrives in an environment where employees feel empowered to explore new ideas, challenge the status quo, and take calculated risks. However, this creative process must be balanced with a strong ethical framework to ensure that innovations are developed and implemented responsibly. Leadership plays a key role in striking this balance by setting clear expectations and guidelines for behavior, while also encouraging experimentation and learning from failures. At Long Beach State University, we constantly sought ways to streamline and improve our business processes. However, as the leader, I made it clear that efficiency should never come at the cost of ethical compromises, such as cutting corners or bypassing necessary approvals.

One of the primary ways that ethical leadership supports innovation is by fostering a culture of transparency and accountability. When leaders are open and honest about their decision-making processes, and take responsibility for the outcomes of their actions, they create a safe space for employees to speak up and share ideas. This open dialogue is essential for identifying potential ethical issues early on, and for ensuring that innovations are developed with consideration for the broader impact on society and the environment.

Ethical leadership promotes innovation by emphasizing the importance of stakeholder engagement and collaboration. By actively seeking out diverse perspectives and involving stakeholders in the innovation process, ethical leaders ensure that new products, services, and processes are developed with a deep understanding of the needs and concerns of all affected parties. This approach not only leads to more successful and sustainable innovations, but also helps build trust and credibility with key stakeholders. As the Athletics Director, much of my efforts focused on stakeholder engagement, to grow philanthropy to the athletics department. This was not a scenario where a donor was purchasing a percentage of the athletics department, but rather philanthropy to enhance and raise the overall student-athlete experience. There is a fine line between investment and ownership, and I did not want to cross a line ethically with any donor.

Ethical innovation is a critical consideration in today's rapidly advancing technological landscape. As groundbreaking technologies emerge, such as artificial intelligence (AI) and gene editing, it is crucial for companies to not only recognize their immense potential for improving human lives but also to carefully evaluate and address the possible unintended consequences and long-term impacts of these innovations.

AI, for example, holds great promise in fields such as healthcare, education, and transportation, with the potential to revolutionize diagnosis and treatment, personalize learning, and enhance road safety. However, AI systems that are developed without proper safeguards can perpetuate biases, violate privacy, and be used for malicious purposes.

Ethical companies have a responsibility to proactively assess and mitigate these risks during the design and development phase of new technologies. This means engaging in rigorous testing, setting up oversight mechanisms, and building in safeguards to prevent misuse or unintended harm. It involves consulting with ethicists, community stakeholders, and industry partners to gain diverse perspectives on the potential impacts of these innovations. If ethical companies fail to proactively assess and mitigate risks during the design and development phase of new technologies, several negative consequences can occur, impacting various stakeholders:

Consumers/End-users: They could be exposed to unforeseen harms such as privacy violations, discrimination, manipulation, or physical injury from unsafe products. Their trust in the company and the technology may be eroded.

Company Reputation: The company's reputation can suffer greatly if their product or service is found to have negative impacts. This potentially leads to loss of customers, decreased sales, and difficulty attracting investors or partners.

Financial Losses: Recalling products, addressing lawsuits, and implementing fixes can be extremely costly. In severe cases, bankruptcy is a possibility.

Employees: Morale can be damaged if employees feel the company is acting unethically. This leads to decreased productivity and higher turnover.

Society: Negative impacts range from widespread misinformation to social inequalities being exacerbated by technology. Trust in technology as a whole can be undermined.

Environment: If environmental risks are not considered, the technology could contribute to pollution, resource depletion, or climate change.

Investors and Shareholders: The financial losses and reputational damage mentioned above directly affect investors and shareholders, leading to decreased stock prices and lower returns on investment.

AI presents a significant ethical dilemma for organizations worldwide, including in my role as Deputy Athletics Director at the University of Washington. AI's potential applications in athletics are vast, from generating game recaps and scouting reports, to crafting broadcast content and even influencing student-athlete recruitment. From a purely cost-benefit perspective, AI seems like a dream: it never sleeps, works tirelessly, and is always available.

However, the ethical implications are substantial. Job displacement is a major concern. If AI takes over tasks previously done by humans, what happens to those individuals? Are they being adequately re-trained and supported in finding new employment? Additionally, the potential for AI to spread misinformation, either for or against the organization, is a real threat. This underscores the crucial point that cheaper doesn't always equate to better, safer, or more trustworthy.

As a leader, it's my responsibility to weigh these ethical considerations against the potential benefits of AI. We must explore ways to harness AI's capabilities while mitigating its potential negative impacts. This involves thoughtful planning, transparent communication, and a commitment to ensuring that the adoption of AI technology aligns with our core values and serves the best interests of our entire community.

It's important to note that the specific impacts and stakeholders affected will vary depending on the nature of the technology and the specific risks involved.

Ethical companies have a responsibility to proactively assess and mitigate risks throughout the entire lifecycle of a technology, starting from the design and development phase. Failure to do so can have far-reaching and damaging consequences for all involved.

By addressing ethical considerations early on, companies help ensure new technologies are developed in a way that maximizes their benefits while minimizing their risks. This proactive approach is far better than dealing with harm after the fact, when the damage may already be done, and public trust could be eroded.

Moreover, by prioritizing ethical innovation, companies differentiate themselves in the market and build a reputation for responsible stewardship of powerful technologies. Consumers, investors, and regulators are increasingly demanding accountability from tech companies, and those that demonstrate a strong ethical framework are more likely to thrive in the long run.

Responsible innovators think deeply about the effects of their creations not just on direct users, but on society as a whole. They engage in ongoing dialogue with ethicists, regulators, and affected communities to surface concerns and incorporate diverse views. They are transparent about their innovation practices and hold themselves accountable for negative outcomes. By instilling ethics at every stage from ideation to implementation, organizations become a force for positive change.

Examples of responsible innovation practices include:
- Conducting thorough ethical reviews of new technologies before deployment.
- Incorporating diverse perspectives in the design and development process.
- Prioritizing sustainability and environmental impact reduction in product design.
- Implement robust privacy and privacy measures.
- Engaging in public dialogue and education about the

potential impacts of new technologies.

By embracing responsible innovation, individuals and organizations are able to contribute to the creation of a more equitable, sustainable, and technologically advanced society.

Overcoming Challenges

In this section, I'd like to address several challenges that arise when prioritizing both ethics and innovation. While striving for ethical innovation is crucial, it's not without its hurdles. In the short term, it can demand tough choices that may disappoint certain stakeholders or require additional investments of time and resources. This means resisting the pressure to compromise on core values or take shortcuts for immediate gains. Ethical issues are rarely straightforward, often involving a complex balancing act between competing interests.

Prioritizing: This involves significant challenges that organizations must navigate thoughtfully. In the short term, prioritizing these values often necessitates making difficult decisions that may disappoint some stakeholders or incur additional costs in terms of time and resources. For instance, adhering to ethical standards might mean rejecting lucrative opportunities that conflict with organizational values or investing in sustainable practices that are more expensive initially.

Resisting pressures to compromise: Turning a blind eye to your values or cutting corners is a constant challenge, especially in competitive industries where the temptation to take the easy route can be strong. Upholding ethical standards requires steadfast commitment from leadership and clear communication of these values throughout the organization. This commitment must be demonstrated through consistent actions and policies that reinforce the importance of ethics over short-term gains.

Complexity of Issues: This often involves competing interests that need to be carefully balanced. For example, a company might face a dilemma between maximizing profits and ensuring fair labor practices, or between rapid product development and thorough safety testing. These decisions are rarely straightforward and require a nuanced understanding of the potential impacts on various stakeholders, including employees, customers, investors, and the broader community.

Continued investment in ethics for the long run: This must come from all levels of an organization. Many organizations struggle with awareness and understanding of how to implement ethical practices effectively. This challenge is often compounded by internal resistance to changing established ways of operating, as employees and leaders may be reluctant to shift from "the way we've always done things."

Limited resources and competing priorities: This can hinder efforts to foster an ethical culture. Organizations often find it difficult to allocate sufficient time, money, and attention to ethics when other pressing issues demand immediate focus. This lack of follow-through could lead to a superficial approach to ethics, where policies exist but are not actively enforced or integrated into daily operations.

Furthermore, industry regulations can add layers of complexity to building an ethical culture, especially for organizations operating across multiple geographies. Different regions may have varying legal requirements and cultural norms, making it challenging to create a cohesive and consistent ethical framework. Navigating these regulatory landscapes requires careful planning and a nuanced understanding of local and international standards.

The Foundations of Ethical Leadership

Ethical leadership extends far beyond mere adherence to rules and regulations. It is a commitment to embodying core values such as integrity, fairness, and respect in every action and decision. Ethical leaders prioritize the long-term well-being of their organization and its stakeholders over short-term gains, understanding that sustainable success is built on a foundation of trust and ethical practices.

This emphasis on long-term benefits was exemplified during my five years at Long Beach State University. I often made decisions that were challenging in the near term but ultimately proved successful in the long run. One such decision was to retain and extend the contract of the Head Coach of the Men's Basketball program. The team had faced a few challenging seasons before my arrival, and there were calls from fans and others to replace the coach.

I spent my first year observing and assessing the coach as well as the program to understand the dynamics before making a decision on his future. I saw a talented coach struggling to find consistent success with his team. In a pivotal conversation, I asked him about his coaching aspirations and the type of players he wanted to coach. His response resonated with me, and we agreed on a new direction for the program. Despite initial criticism, I extended his contract for another five years.

This decision ultimately paid off. In my final year at Long Beach State, the Men's Basketball team won the Big West Conference and made the postseason. The following season, they repeated their conference victory and even secured a spot in the NCAA Tournament. While the short-term challenges were significant, the long-term benefits of this ethical decision were undeniable.

Fostering a culture of transparency, where open communication is encouraged and information is shared freely, is another hallmark of ethical leadership. This empowers teams to make informed decisions and contribute to the organization's collective success. Additionally, ethical leaders hold themselves and their teams accountable for their actions, ensuring that any ethical lapses are addressed promptly and constructively. This commitment to accountability not only strengthens the organization's ethical foundation but also creates a shared sense of responsibility among all members, further reinforcing a culture of integrity.

As an ethical leader, I practice open and honest communication with all coaches, staff, and student-athletes ensuring everyone knows where they stand and understands the expectations and assessment criteria on how "end of year" and "end of season" reviews would be conducted. This transparency fostered a culture of trust and accountability, contributing to the overall success of the athletic program.

The Path Forward

The journey toward ethical leadership and innovation is ongoing. It requires a constant commitment to learning, adaptation, and self-reflection. By embracing these principles, you can not only drive business success but also contribute to a more sustainable and equitable future for all.

In summary, fostering an ethical culture demands a sustained and multifaceted effort. Organizations must be proactive in raising awareness, overcoming internal resistance, allocating adequate resources, and navigating regulatory complexities to ensure that ethical practices are truly embedded in their operations.

The pace of technological change makes it difficult for ethical thinking to keep up. By the time an innovation's full implications are understood, it may already be widely deployed. Ethical innovators have to anticipate issues before they become crises and build in precautionary measures from the start. This demands a willingness to ask tough questions, consider worst case scenarios, and potentially delay or forgo deploying innovations that pose unreasonable risks.

Responsible innovation may require uncomfortable transparency, such as admitting mistakes, sharing data, or incorporating critical feedback. Some firms may be reluctant to adopt practices that competitors don't follow, fearing it could put them at a disadvantage. A pervasive misconception is that ethics and innovation are incompatible, when in fact they are mutually reinforcing.

However, the advantages of ethical innovative leadership far outweigh any challenges. By building trust, organizations gain lasting competitive advantages - devoted customers, engaged employees, collaborative partners, and community support. A reputation for integrity attracts top talent and creates brand equity.

Principled companies make thoughtful decisions that benefit all stakeholders and society. They are more resilient in weathering any storms that do arise. Most importantly, ethical organizations make a meaningful positive difference in people's lives and the world.

In an era of accelerating change, eroding trust, and rising societal expectations, ethics has never been more urgent for business success. Companies that earn trust through unwavering integrity and responsible innovation are best positioned to thrive long-term. By anchoring themselves in strong moral principles while unceasingly pursuing progress, they not only drive financial results but contribute to building a better world. The new bottom line is enhancing the lives of all stakeholders and uplifting society.

As innovative technologies transform our world at breakneck speed, steadfast ethics must be the rudder that steers progress toward its highest potential. When human-centered values guide each breakthrough, we harness the best of invention while protecting against its risks. From AI to genetic engineering, proactively instilling integrity maximizes the promise and minimizes the perils.

Whether at the cutting edge of innovation or in day-to-day operations, the core principles of ethical leadership endure. Treat others with respect. Make decisions as if the whole world is watching. When the choice is difficult, ask not what you can get away with, but what you would be proud to stand behind. Measure success not just by outcomes but by the rightness of the path to achieve them.

Practical Takeaways for Leaders and Innovators

Incorporate ethics into your core values and mission statement: Clearly define your organization's ethical principles and ensure they are integrated into all aspects of your operations.

Lead by example: Demonstrate ethical behavior in your own actions and decisions. Be transparent about your decision-making processes and hold yourself accountable to the highest standards.

Encourage open communication: Create a safe space for employees to voice concerns, share ideas, and raise ethical questions. Promote a culture of trust and transparency.

Embrace diversity and inclusion: Seek out diverse perspectives and encourage employees from different backgrounds to contribute to the innovation process.

Engage with stakeholders: Listen to the needs and concerns of your customers, employees, suppliers, and community members. Involve them in your innovation efforts.

Measure and report your impact: Track your social and

environmental impact, communicating it transparently to your stakeholders.

Support ethical initiatives: Invest in programs and initiatives that promote social and environmental responsibility. Advocate policies supporting ethical business practices.

By embracing ethical leadership and fostering a culture of innovation, you create a resilient, successful, and impactful organization that contributes to a better world. The B Corp model offers a valuable framework for integrating ethical considerations into every aspect of your business, from product development to supply chain management to employee engagement.

These timeless ideals, lived out in the thousands of choices that make up our days, are the seeds from which ethical cultures blossom. As those seeds spread, the harvest is trust, goodwill, resilience, and positive impact - a renewable source of strength to draw on in times of trial and uncertainty.

The road of ethical leadership is not always smooth or simple. Looking back at my journey from my first year to my final year at Long Beach State University, I see a leader who evolved and learned to apply valuable lessons gained through experience. Balancing competing interests, resisting short-term pressures, and making hard calls that benefit the greater good demand courage, foresight and perseverance. But this is the defining work of our time. In rising to the challenge, today's leaders have the opportunity and responsibility to shape a future in which technology and human values uplift each other, integrity and ingenuity are inextricably intertwined, and business is a powerful engine for sustainable prosperity.

The 21st century demands nothing less than a revolution in business where innovation is celebrated but character is non-negotiable, profits and principles fuel each other, and the ultimate goal is not just to do well, but to do immeasurable good. It falls to each of us to be the vanguards of that revolution through our own unflinching commitment to ethics and ceaseless striving for better. In each decision we face, we must choose the harder right over the easier wrong. Only then can we unleash the full power of human enterprise to tackle the great challenges of our time.

By coupling groundbreaking creativity with unshakeable integrity, companies can be an unstoppable force for positive transformation. When innovation is the engine and ethics the compass, business has the ability to take us to extraordinary new heights and touch more lives than ever before. The journey starts now. The rewards – for organizations and the world – are boundless. Ethics and innovation, hand in hand, pave the path to a brighter tomorrow. I encourage each of you to take that crucial first step!

About Andy Fee

Deputy Athletics Director, Seattle University

Meet Andy Fee, the dynamic Deputy Athletics Director for Seattle University's Redhawk Sports. Joining the team in August 2024, Andy's mission is all about boosting revenue, rallying public support, and shining a spotlight on Seattle U's sports programs.  With a keen eye for strategy, he's in charge of everything from marketing and fan experiences to corporate partnerships and major capital projects.

Before making waves at Seattle U, Andy was the Deputy Athletics Director & Chief of Staff at the University of Washington. There, he played a pivotal role in Husky Football's journey to the NCAA CFP National Championship and helped guide the Men's Rowing team to their 20th National Championship. Managing a hefty $161 million budget for 22 Division I programs, Andy's leadership extended across sport administration, student-athlete wellness, and even the university's renowned rowing and basketball teams.

Andy's career also includes a successful stint as Executive Director of Athletics at Long Beach State University, where he oversaw the construction of a $16 million Soccer/Softball Clubhouse and celebrated two NCAA National Championships in men's volleyball.

Off the field, Andy enjoys life on his 54-foot boat in Seattle's Portage Bay with his wife, Nicole, and their dog, Winston.

Socially Responsible Leadership

By Natalie Parks, PhD, BCBA-D, LP

In the landscape of corporate leadership, a new paradigm is emerging—one that demands more than just profit-driven decision-making. This chapter delves into the realm of socially responsible leadership, a critical component of the modern C-Suite. Like a captain navigating a pirate ship through treacherous waters to find the invaluable treasure, today's leaders must steer their organizations toward success while simultaneously addressing pressing social and environmental concerns. The treasure for leaders is not gold doubloons; however, it's a happy, inclusive, high-performing team that sees you as a hero and beacon of hope in the world of social justice. Sounds like a lot? Well, it is. But don't worry, I've got you covered. Let's embark on this journey together to uncover the treasure of the seven keys of socially responsible leadership.

Now, before you start thinking, "How on Earth do I do that?" Let's break it down. In over 20 years of experience in leadership, I have learned the secret to navigating the roughest waters. I call it my seven keys to socially responsible leadership. Now these aren't just any ordinary brass trinket keys - they're the mystical tools of a true captain of social responsibility. Think of them as your nautical charts, sextant, and enchanted compass all rolled into one. They'll guide you to uncharted islands of inclusivity, help you navigate the treacherous reefs of bias, and unlock treasure chests brimming with untapped potential in your crew. With these keys in hand, you'll transform your vessel into a legendary ship of opportunity, where every sailor, regardless of their background, can hoist their true colors and contribute to the journey. You'll be the Captain Jack Sparrow of the corporate world - savvy enough to outwit the most daunting challenges, minus the rum (unless you fancy a tot, but that's a different kind of leadership altogether).

What is Socially Responsible Leadership?

Let's get real. Socially responsible leadership isn't just about looking good on paper or ticking the right boxes. It's about real, actionable change that benefits not just your team, but society as a whole. It's about recognizing the power dynamics at play, understanding your own privilege, and using that awareness to lift others up. It's about creating an environment where everyone can thrive – because this is the only workplace that will continue to thrive in the ever-changing, fast paced world of today and the future.

The Seven Keys

Leading a team can be like herding cats. And leading a socially responsible team? That's like herding cats while juggling flaming torches and riding a unicycle. It's tricky but totally doable with the right skills and a sense of humor. And with practical, intentional actions, you can start moving away from herding cats toward leaving a legacy of doing good and unlocking the true potential of your entire team.

As we dive into these seven keys, remember that this isn't a one-time checklist. It's an ongoing process of growth and learning. You'll make mistakes (we all do), but the goal is to keep moving forward, keep striving for better, and keep making a difference. And hey, if you mess up, just remember even the best chefs burned a couple of souffles along the way.

Are you ready to become the leader who inspires and transforms? If so, buckle up because we're about to embark on a journey through the Seven Keys to Socially Responsible Leadership. It's going to be informative; it's going to be transformative, and hey, it might be even a little fun. Let's do this!

Key 1: Embrace Inclusivity

Picture this: you're a small child, full of excitement about the new wooden train track you just received. You've got all the different pieces – the straight ones, the curvy ones, a bridge, and tunnels. Your goal? To make the most epic, mind-blowingly awesome train track the world has ever seen. You get to work and just as you are adding the final piece of your creation, you look to your left and see a piece sitting all by itself in the corner. You sigh, look at the track that is your masterpiece, and back at the piece in the corner. A track just isn't right if you leave a piece out! It's almost like cheating. You take another slow, deep breath and take the track apart. It's time to start again.

Inclusion is a bit like that wooden train track. When done right, all the pieces fit together smoothly, and the track is seamless. However, when it's not done right, the pieces can be strained, and the track becomes bumpy. And while your track would have worked just fine leaving that last piece in the corner where it was, deep down, you know it's not the right solution.

As you would have read previously in this book: In the workplace, our communities, and relationships, inclusion is about valuing the unique contributions, perspectives, and experiences of every individual. It's about being willing to rearrange the "track" of our preconceptions and biases to create a space where everyone can thrive.

Of course, it may take extra effort at times and even a bit of creative problem-solving. We might have to challenge the way we've done things or have some uncomfortable conversations. But just like with the train track, the end result is worth it: a stronger, more vibrant, more innovative, and more complete whole (Hunt et al., 2015).

Inclusion is not easy and there are many subtle behaviors that create an exclusive environment, even when the best intentions are in place. Embracing inclusivity demands more than mere tolerance or acceptance - it requires recognizing that diverse perspectives actively enrich and strengthen the team. That's not all; leadership also requires one to model behaviors that demonstrate this recognition each and every day. Here are a few things that help increase your inclusion of others:

Review Policies and Practices: Equitable policies and practices increase performance of all employees (Bernstein et al., 2021). Ensure they promote diversity and inclusion. Use gender-neutral language. Ensure fairness in performance evaluations by providing measurable and observable targets (Elkhwesky et al., 2021).

Seek Diverse Viewpoints: Diverse groups increase organizational innovation and financial results (Levine, 2020). Actively gather perspectives from multiple team members to avoid one-sided decisions. Create teams of individuals with different backgrounds, strengths and skills, and perspectives.

Review hiring and promotional practices: Bias in hiring practices remains unchanged since the 1990s for some groups (Alabi & Mahmuda, 2024; Chen, 2023). Create scoring rubrics that are behaviorally anchored and measurable to use during interviews. Monitor hiring and promotions to reveal any biases. Evaluate the applicant pool to determine if you are hiring across the same diversity of the applicants.

Create psychological safety: Psychological safety in the workplace results in team members speaking up, taking risks, and sharing information and can have incredible impacts on goal attainment (Edmondson & Bransby, 2023). Complete check-in rounds every meeting (e.g., what was the weather like for work this week - stormy, sunny, rain & sun, cloudy). Invite quieter people to speak up by going first when sharing. Ban interruptions.

Communicate inclusively: Inclusive communication enables as many people as possible to be included in the interaction (Brce & Kogovšek, 2020). Communicate openly and honestly. Use team-oriented language (us, we). Consider other perspectives and choose words that are respectful to everyone.

Address microaggressions immediately: Miroaggressions are statements, questions, and assumptions that are offensive and signal a bias towards someone, usually without the person making the statement realizing it. The impact of these are plentiful including high blood pressure and depression (Parks et al., 2024). Educate yourself on microaggressions so you can easily recognize when they occur. Stop them when observed. Empower your team to do the same. If you make a microaggression, apologize and correct your mistake.

Inclusion fosters a culture in which each person feels valued and respected, leading to increased motivation, innovation, and collaboration. It is not something that you can master and be done with. However, inclusion is a skill that needs to be practiced and strengthened each and every day. Just like when you begin to work out after a long hiatus, getting into the routine of things can be exhausting and cause some pain. But once you are in the routine, growth gets easier, you become stronger, and you are able to help others on their journey as well.

So next time you're building a train track (or navigating the complexities of inclusion in your own life), remember: every piece matters. Be willing to shift and adjust, or even completely restart, to make room for everyone.

Key 2: Cultivate Self-Awareness and Humility

Most leaders tell me they are great at being self-aware and practicing humility. Several years ago, I was one of those leaders too.

Picture this: I was 31, leading a team of just under 30 people, and feeling pretty good about myself. I mean, I was building strong relationships, being inclusive, had a really awesome, hard-working team - the whole nine yards. But then, one day, I made a mis-judged comment referencing Nazis. I know, not my finest moment.

Looking back, I'm mortified at how short-sighted and insensitive I was. But at that moment, I was clueless. It wasn't until later that day when one of my team members came to me and shared her family's story. Her grandparents had survived concentration camps, branded with numbers, and then made it to the US. She knew me well enough to know I didn't mean any harm, but my words had struck a chord, reminding her of the unimaginable trauma her family had endured.

Let's be real - she was way nicer about it than I deserved, and it was only because of the positive relationships I'd built that I didn't completely torpedo my credibility as a leader. But here's the thing: none of that matters. My intent, my lack of insight - it's all irrelevant. What matters is that I left one of my team members feeling isolated and unsupported, and that's on me.

That's where humility comes in. When my team member shared her family's history with me, I had a choice. I could get defensive, doubling down on my mistake, or I could embrace the opportunity to grow. I chose the latter. I admitted my mistake, apologized sincerely, and committed to doing better.

That moment taught me a valuable lesson: no matter how great we think we are; we all have room for improvement. Cultivating self-awareness and humility isn't about beating ourselves up for our mistakes; it's about recognizing that we're human, we're going to mess up sometimes, and that's okay. What matters is how we respond when we do.

Let this be a reminder to all of us. Build those strong relationships, be inclusive, but don't forget to check yourself along the way. And when you inevitably stick your foot in your mouth (because let's face it, we all do), embrace the opportunity to learn, grow, and do better. Your team (and your conscience) will thank you for it.

Key 3: Build Genuine Connections

Let's face it: some people just click with you, while others can really get under your skin. But when you're leading a team, you don't get to pick and choose who you work with. Avoiding the "pineapple pizza" people (you know, the ones you find disagreeable or off-putting) might be tempting, but it's not exactly inclusive, is it?

What's a leader to do with those hard-to-work-with team members? Build genuine connections with them! When people feel connected, they feel valued. They trust you, they trust each other, and they're more likely to bring their A-game to the table. Plus, when you're focused on building those genuine connections, you might find the things that once drove you crazy about your colleagues don't seem quite so bad anymore. You might even start to see their quirks as a strength to the team.

How do you actually go about building these connections? Here are some strategies:

Create opportunities for meaningful dialogue and team building: Make space for authentic conversations and experiences that help you get to know each other as people, not just as coworkers. Add 'check ins' as part of meeting agendas or have morning coffee meetings. One supervisor used to walk to the gas station across the street for quick breaks and sodas. He invited his team members to go, which created space for dialogue outside of work meetings.

Show genuine interest in the well-being and development of each team member: Everyone wants to feel valued by their leaders. A great way to do this is to check in regularly, learn about their personal goals and create opportunities for them to advance and learn - even if it doesn't always directly benefit the team.

Practice active listening and seek to understand others' experiences: Active listening shows you value the person communicating. Put down the phone, make eye contact, and ask questions to gain a deeper understanding.

Communicate transparently and regularly: Communication is the best way to keep everyone aware of what is occurring and increase their inclusion in the organization. Keep your team informed about project updates, changes in the company, and anything else that might impact them.

Be Vulnerable: Sharing personal struggles and insecurities can deepen your connection with team members and peers (Franco, 2022). Ditch the typical small talk at the beginning of meetings and ask more meaningful questions like "what's the last thing you learned?", "what's one way you hope to grow this year?" or "what is one obstacle you faced recently?"

Take my relationship with one of my colleagues, for example. We took a test about how we show up at work, and let's just say we couldn't be more different. I'm all about getting things done and analyzing every little detail, while he's more of a "people first, processes later" kind of guy. Initially we bumped heads, him feeling frustrated that I rarely took the time to check in with him or ask about his children, and me frustrated that he was always "off task" and not concerned about getting through our agenda. Once we took time to learn our priorities and put strategies in place to fill both our needs, everything changed. We started having regular check-ins, practicing active listening, and keeping each other in the loop. The result? A genuine connection that not only made our work together better but made coming to the office a whole lot more enjoyable.

Building genuine connections takes effort, but it's worth it. You'll build a team that trusts each other, values each other, and knocks it out the park every time. And who knows? You might just find that pineapple on pizza isn't so bad after all.

Key 4: Provide Effective and Constructive Feedback

Feedback is my thing. I am obsessed with it because it can make or break a relationship in an instant. Delivered correctly, feedback is a powerful and cost-effective tool that results in increases in performance, inclusion, and happiness with the organization (Ventura et al., 2020). Used wrongly, it can destroy a relationship and literally push the person out of the organization.

Let me illustrate with a quick story. One of my clients, Cori, led a small team of managers. She was working with me to increase her leadership skills as well as her inclusion of diverse individuals. One of Cori's main goals was to increase the team feeling with her managers and to remove the hierarchical structure that typically exists between managers and their supervisors. One day her unit was completing professional development workshops in the afternoon. Each manager was to lead a small group of their team members. There was one team in particular Cori was most concerned about, so she chose Fran, her most experienced and dependable manager, to lead it. Fran was also the manager she had the closest relationship with. Mid-morning, Fran headed to Cori's office, but met her in the hallway. Fran told Cori that she completely forgot to highlight that she had the afternoon off. She was leaving work in an hour and would miss the workshops that afternoon.

Cori's response? "As your manager, I need to know these things early so that I can plan for them."

Now let's pause the story for a second. Remember that Cori was working to create a team atmosphere and that she not only relied more on Fran than others, but she was also closer to Fran personally. Cori all but destroyed this with that one statement. She received a scathing email from Fran that night. Fran stated that she felt devalued, 'put in her place', and nothing like a team member. She also wrote that she felt Cori didn't even personally care about her. Their strong relationship was all but destroyed.

Luckily Cori was humble enough to recognize her grave mistake and met with Fran the next day. She apologized, listened, validated everything Fran shared, and discussed a path forward. They were able to recover their relationship, but it did take some time and deliberate actions from Cori to rebuild that trust and move the entire team past the hierarchy she had been working so hard to decrease.

If only Cori had followed a few simple rules to provide effective and constructive feedback, the fall out could have been avoided.

First and foremost, feedback should always focus on the behavior or outcome, not the person. It's not about pointing fingers or making someone feel bad. It's about identifying what needs to be improved and why it matters. Cori's feedback that began with "as your manager" immediately points fingers and reinforces that she has authority over Fran. Instead, Cori should have highlighted the impact of Fran leaving on short notice. It leaves a team without a leader and very little time for planning around this.

Next, be specific. Don't just say "this is wrong". Explain the exact issue. Then help fix it. Provide information on how to correct any errors that are discussed and ensure the person has the opportunity to ask questions or even practice when appropriate. This ensures the correction sticks the next time the same task is performed. The example above is simple here. Cori should first state the impact of Fran's behavior. Let her know that helping to plan a workshop and lead a team, then all of a sudden remembering you will be out on very short notice, leaves the team without a leader. It is unfair on the team. In the future, please let us know as soon as possible if you have timing conflicts with big projects and training sessions. Giving us notice at the beginning of planning would be even better.

In addition to corrective feedback, leaders should get really good at providing positive feedback. In fact, teams that receive more positive as opposed to corrective feedback are more likely to go above and beyond consistently. Positive feedback should still focus on the behavior and be specific, which makes others believe you are genuine and not just trying to inflate their ego for your own benefit. Cori had to focus a lot on positive feedback after her mistake. Even in the follow up conversation, Cori thanked Fran for sharing her thoughts and having the courage to be open and honest. She also thanked Fran for listening and helping to find a path forward. The next time Fran was off, she told Cori immediately and put it in the calendar. Cori again provided positive feedback for this.

The last thing to remember about feedback is that you should be able to receive it just as well as you give it. Create an environment where your team feels they are safe to provide you with feedback just as easily and frequently as you provide them with feedback. This will not only increase the morale of your team, but also make you a better leader. It is those who follow you who know best how your behavior affects performance. Listen to the advice they give! While Cori did many things wrong in this situation, she soared here. There is evidence she created an environment where her team was comfortable in sharing negative and corrective feedback with her. And when she received it, Cori did the best thing; she accepted it, owned her mistakes, and listened to the advice Fran gave about how to do better next time.

Key 5: Empower and Invest in Others

Empowering and investing in others is not just good for your team, it is a complete game-changer.

One client of mine provides the perfect example. Susan is a business owner of an organization that provides diversity, equity, and inclusion training to other organizations. Susan meets Olufunmilayo (Olu) at a conference. Olu is a rockstar in her field but feels a bit stuck in her current gig. Susan sees an opportunity and offers Olu a chance to flex her skills with some training workshops for Susan's company. Olu is thrilled - extra cash and a chance to branch out? Sign her up!

Fast forward a few months, there have been a couple of changes in the company. The organization has grown, and Susan is looking for additional avenues of service to invest in. Olu has expressed a desire to begin a line of services of her own, so her and Susan begin conversations regarding Olu joining the company permanently.

Ultimately, Susan makes an offer to Olu that will help her with administrative tasks and marketing, allowing Olu to focus on the delivery of her services. This would be an excellent opportunity for the business and for Olu. But in a meeting, Susan and Olu have a heart-to-heart, where Susan realizes that while the offer will be great for her company, it may not actually be the best thing for Olu and her long-term goals. Susan advises Olu to turn down the offer. Talk about putting your team first! Wow!

Now, let's break this down. Susan could have done several things when she had her heart-to-heart with Olu. Knowing how much Olu liked and respected her, she could have tried to influence her to join the company. She could have chosen not to offer any advice and allowed Olu to figure it out herself. But she offered the best advice she could give, the advice that invests in Olu. Investing in your team isn't about creating a sense of obligation or pulling strings for personal gain. That's not leadership; that's just shady. True leaders invest in their team's growth and advancement, no strings attached. Sure, some might outgrow the company and move on, but guess what? They'll be singing your praises and sending their talented friends your way. And the ones who stick around will be loyal, engaged, and ready to crush it. To date, Olu has sent more contractors and business to the company than any other person.

Empowering your team isn't just good for them; it's good for you too! When you give your team the tools, mentorship, and autonomy they need to shine, you're freeing up your own plate to focus on the big-picture stuff. It's like having a bunch of mini leaders running around, solving problems and collaborating like pros.

The first thing you need to do to make this happen is to get to know your team's goals and aspirations. What makes them tick? Where do they want to be in 10 years? Then provide opportunities that align with their goals. Make sure you're giving everyone a fair shot, especially those from underrepresented groups. Encourage autonomy by clearly defining what decisions they can make without you and give them a virtual high-five when they do. And finally, delegate, delegate, delegate! Don't be afraid to delegate the juicy projects either. Give your team a chance to step up and watch them soar!

Investing in and empowering your team is a win-win-win. Your team grows, your company thrives, and you get to sit back and watch it all happen. Just remember, it's not about creating a bunch of mini-mes or holding people hostage with favors. It's about nurturing a team of confident, capable, and loyal rockstars who will have your back, even if they end up moving on to bigger and better things.

Key 6: Challenge Your Bias and Create Equity

Let's face it - we all have bias. Sometimes these biases are harmless, but other times they can result in inequitable opportunities for our team. Leaders who regularly evaluate their behaviors, look for their own biases, and work to ensure an equitable workplace have teams who are more diverse and innovative, and organizations that are more profitable.

Zaria was a supervisor at a small company of physical therapists. Sariyah was one of four interns at the company, all of whom worked directly under Zaria's supervision. Sariyah began having difficulty about three months into her practicum and noticed that she was not being offered the same opportunities as the other three interns. She spoke to Zaria about her concerns only to be brushed off and told that Sariyah had chosen slightly different things to focus on than the other three and that was why their experiences were different. Sariyah wasn't convinced this was the case and finally discussed the situation with one of her professors.

During discussion, Sariyah's professor paused and said "It seems there is something you are not telling me. Is there something you want to say, but you are concerned about the outcome if you voice it?" Sariyah sighed and hesitantly told her professor that she thought Zaria could be biased against her. She was the only African American in the entire organization and while she didn't think she was being discriminated against, she did feel that the relationship with Zaria and the lack of opportunities may have something to do with a negative bias against her based on her race.

Upon investigation, it was found that there were other African American females who had a difficult time with Zaria and while none of them could speak to specific forms of discrimination, all felt they were given different opportunities and all ended up transitioning away from the organization.

When asked, Zaria did what many well-meaning leaders do and cited her best friend, who is African American. She dug in and defended her choices, refusing to believe that she had any biases that could affect her work with interns.

Zaria is not unique, and this story is not to pick on all the Zaria's of the world. It's already been stated that every one of us has biases. What I want to highlight here is that the problem arises when we focus more on denying our biases than on examining their presence and ensuring that our behavior does not lead to inequitable opportunities for certain individuals or groups. Leaders who pay attention to their own behaviors, to their thoughts about others, and to how others are interacting with them are more likely to identify their own biases and catch them before they have a negative impact on others. Additionally, these leaders review data to ensure biases are not common practice in the organization as a whole – and if they are, they work to change policies and procedures to eliminate them.

So, what can we do as leaders to decrease the likeliness bias will negatively affect our teams?

Review hiring practices: Even very small amounts of bias can produce significant rates of discrimination when hiring, and productivity loss (Hardy et al., 2022). Hiring practices should be reviewed to ensure applicants are diverse, hires represent the applicant pool, and promotions reflect the employee pool. Any time one group is interviewed, hired, or promoted more than others, bias is likely present.

Speak up regularly and openly about bias: Talking about bias decreases the stigma and invites more inclusion (Parks et al., 2024). Model discussions of bias openly call out microaggressions and make inclusion a part of daily discussions and practices.

Display humility when receiving feedback: As stated above, receiving feedback empowers team members and increases productivity. This means you will likely hear things that are uncomfortable and that you may not agree with. Invite feedback regarding your performance, and especially your biases. When you receive feedback, thank the person, and act on it.

Include multiple perspectives in decision-making: The most innovative teams are highly diverse. When making decisions, gather diverse viewpoints. Challenge teams that immediately agree with suggestions and set the expectation that disagreement and differences of perspective and opinion are the norm.

The honest fact is that we cannot eliminate bias, and not everything will be equitable. We don't live in a perfect world. However, leaders can work to create equitable opportunities for others by identifying the individuals or groups who are less likely to be offered opportunities and then offering to them first. They can work to eliminate their own bias by observing their own behaviors and thoughts and asking for honest and open feedback from their team.

The result? Inclusive and equitable teams and workplaces have employees who are more innovative, happier, and more likely to go above and beyond, resulting in more productivity and higher profits in the end.

Key 7: Lead with a Legacy Mindset

Never has a leader said, "I want to be remembered as a complete jerk." Let's face it, as a leader, you want others to remember the good you did for them and the organization. The unfortunate truth is that too many leaders go down in history as "bad leaders" because they missed the mark on the seven keys to socially responsible leadership. This final key completes the set by aligning your behavior (what you do and say) with the lasting impression you want to leave long after you've exited.

Take a moment to think about three of the greatest leaders you know. Write down 5-10 things they do that set them apart. Then ask yourself how many of these things are part of your daily practice?

If you're not quite there yet, don't worry – there's still time. Leading with a legacy mindset is not something you do just once, it is a way of living your life, showing up to work each day. It doesn't mean that you are perfect and don't have bad days – or make mistakes (even big mistakes). It means that in general, you spend your days focused on these:

Vision: Have a clear, compelling vision for the future. Anticipate future trends and opportunities and inspire others to work towards it. Visionary leaders tie the specific duties of each member of the team to the larger vision of the organization, stressing the importance of every team member in achieving the organization's goal.

Integrity: Be honest, ethical, and consistent in their words and actions. Do what is right even when others are not around and focus on building trust with and between the team.

Resilience: Overcome difficulties quickly. Don't let bumps in the road detract you from the goal. Approach problems with a solution-focused orientation and leave the past there. Learn from mistakes and use this learning the next time problems arise.

Accountability: State when you are wrong, without waiting for someone to point it out. Ensure that no team members get away with everything, holding all to the same standards.

Inclusive Communication: Communicate for understanding, practicing active listening and give careful consideration to the words you use. Consider how your message might be received by each person, ensuring your communication brings people together rather than dividing them.

Lifelong Learning: Constantly learn new things, whether from reading, attending workshops and conferences, or from your staff. Openly share what you have learned and create a pathway for all to share their expertise.

Commitment to Social Justice: Focus on fairness and equity in your organization and larger society. Work to dismantle and change unfair practices, creating a legacy of positive social change and inclusivity.

Bringing it all together

Leadership is about people. It's about understanding that each person brings unique strengths, perspectives, and experiences to the table, and it's our job as leaders to create an environment where those differences are not just accepted but celebrated. It's about recognizing your own biases and privileges, using that awareness to foster a culture of equity and inclusion, and watching your team come alive.

Being a socially responsible leader isn't about perfection, it's about progress. It's about showing up every day with the intention to do better, to be better, and to make a positive difference in the lives of those around us. It's about having the courage to confront our own shortcomings, the humility to learn from others, and the vision to create a brighter future for all.

As you continue on your own leadership journey, remember that these seven keys to socially responsible leadership are not just a checklist to be completed, but rather a compass to orient and guide you towards a more inclusive, equitable, and impactful way of leading. The path is not always easy and can be the road less traveled. You'll face challenges, setbacks, and humbling moments along the way. But with persistence, compassion, and a healthy dose of humor, you have the power to create a legacy that will inspire others for years to come.

Your journey to becoming a socially responsible leader starts now. Embrace the keys, transform your team, and lead with purpose. The world is waiting for your impact!

About Dr. Natalie Parks, Ph.D., BCBA-D

CEO of Dr. Natalie Inc. & Co-Owner of Behavior Leader LLC and Accelerate Bx LLC

Meet Dr. Natalie Parks, a trailblazer in psychology and behavior analysis dedicated to creating a more just and equitable society.

She's the author of key works like The Behavior of Social Justice: Applying Behavior Analysis to Understand and Challenge Injustice, and has contributed to influential publications on leadership and culturally responsive practices.

Her books, Leadership in Behavior Analysis and Feedback F!@#ups and How to Solve Them, highlight her deep understanding of effective leadership and organizational dynamics.

As the CEO of Dr. Natalie Inc. and co-owner of Behavior Leader LLC and Accelerate Bx LLC, Dr. Parks is on a mission to disrupt systems of social injustice using behavioral science.

Her commitment to creating inclusive environments is reflected in her teaching, coaching, and leadership initiatives. Recognized with the Martin Luther King Jr. Spirit Award for her dedication to racial unity, Dr. Parks continues to inspire change and champion social justice through her research and advocacy.

Impactful Leadership

By Paula Valle Castañon

Strive for Positive Impact Through Actions

In a traditional work environment, we often enter a room believing that leaders are the individuals in authority positions, the ones with the important titles, or those who hold all the power. However, true leadership is not confined to titles or positions. Instead, it involves being a guiding light that offers direction and clarity, especially during challenging times.

Embracing a Civil Leadership Model requires leaders to step away from traditional models of leadership and learn to put people first. In this model, a leader doesn't lead through hierarchical power, but through earning their teams' trust by showing up with care and support.

No matter your title, age, gender, education, or salary, YOU ARE A LEADER, and you can have a positive impact in your organization, effect meaningful change at work, or within your community, while staying true to yourself.

Cultivating future leaders that rely on empathy, listening, stewardship, and commitment to personal growth rather than a title to lead is when true transformation in a workplace occurs. Listening to your team members and showing that you value their input can alone boost their engagement by 24 percent. When employees in a corporate environment are highly engaged, they outperform their peers by 147 percent in profits per share.

Leadership is not just about directing people or delegating work to junior staff. It isn't about minimizing staff or treating individuals as disposable. Leadership is about inspiring others, providing guidance, mentorship, listening, and staying open to new ideas and ways of doing things. Effective leadership creates an atmosphere where everyone feels committed to the team, mission, or even simply to one another, and can improve team performance by up to 30 percent. The best team results I have ever achieved have been when I was able to bring everyone together and make them feel that they were valued, trusted, and heard.

The Importance of Support and Guidance

I recently counseled a young woman on how to navigate difficult work situations. Sophie was starting out in her career and had been given an assignment with limited guidance or direction. Her supervisor said that he would prepare a comprehensive brief on the software program he wanted her to learn before he went out on leave. Regrettably, her supervisor went on a three-month leave without providing her with the promised brief or any additional guidance. Sophie felt frustrated, overwhelmed, and out of her element with the task she had been given. When she turned to her acting supervisor to ask for help and support, she was told to figure it out for herself. Have you ever been in that situation? How did you approach having a project that you felt was over your head and your supervisors were not offering you the support or answers that you were hoping to hear?

In Sophie's case, she attempted to learn the required platform through tutorials. Unfortunately, when she failed to meet her supervisor's deadline for mastering the platform, her anticipated promotion was postponed. She felt punished for her supervisor's lack of support and didn't understand how to succeed, especially after seeking help from leadership and trying to learn the platform on her own.

Her supervisor, rather than creating a space of mentorship and guidance, did the exact opposite, which made her feel unsupported, unmotivated, and discouraged. Ultimately, she quit her job.

The Ripple Effect of Leadership Choices

Sophie was a vital member of the team, as the only individual with her technical skillset at their organization. Her supervisor's lack of support was shortsighted. Rather than provide clarity or give her an extension, he withheld an expected promotion to motivate her. His approach failed and resulted in Sophie leaving. Her supervisor did try to convince her to stay, knowing that hiring a replacement would be costly and time-consuming. But it was too late.

Her departure highlighted a failure in leadership. This is a common theme I have seen over the course of my career. Team members rely on their leaders for support and direction. By not providing the tools Sophie needed to succeed, her supervisors created an environment that failed to foster commitment to the team or organization.

Why Should We Care?

What would have occurred had leadership given her the support she asked for? Had leadership provided the necessary support they could have developed a loyal junior staff member, saved time and money, and inspired at least one person.

This situation highlights the importance of seeking mentorship and leadership from other sources when your supervisor isn't providing the support you need. While Sophie could have approached her request for help differently, or learned the program in another way, her inexperience made it difficult to navigate those challenges without proper guidance or coaching.

When leaders work with individuals who are just starting their careers, they have a unique opportunity to foster growth and learning. As a leader, don't miss an opportunity to provide direction and develop talented staff, because those are future supervisors and leaders. If you are just starting out in your career, do not be afraid to seek outside mentorship when your supervisor misses the mark.

Reflecting on Leadership

As leaders, we sometimes miss our goals. In those instances, it's valuable to reflect on the situation and think about how you could approach it differently next time and consider what advice you would offer to someone navigating similar challenges.

The kind of treatment and leadership you would want to see in others is something you should model yourself.

Impactful leadership is not about impacting everyone. It may be about impacting your team, one staff member, a customer, an external partner, or even yourself in a positive way. Don't minimize what leadership looks like, or what impact it can have.

The Impact of Leading by Example

One constant you will hear from any team member that I have led is that I will never ask or expect my team to do something that I wouldn't do myself. If we need to stay up until 1:00 am to set-up or breakdown for an event, a press conference, or update graphics, I will be right there with them. I firmly believe that building a team means never considering oneself too superior to engage in grunt work or mundane tasks.

I cannot say this enough: you must model the behavior you want to see from your team, your leaders, and other staff. Someone is always watching your actions. By modeling integrity, respect, and empathy, you impact how others choose to lead and break toxic leadership archetypes. You have the power to develop and create new leaders – no matter what your title is.

Have you ever worked at a corporation or organization where the President or CEO led by fear and intimidation? How did you feel in that environment? Did you feel committed to the mission or vision? Would you say you felt loyalty to that individual or organization?

The answers may seem obvious. This kind of environment fosters mistrust, resentment, low employee morale, and leads to a breakdown in productivity, teamwork and collaboration. People typically stay in a job where fear is the driving force because they can't afford to leave. Meanwhile, they are suffering mentally and physically under constant fear that they might lose their job.

When people are under this fear, they're not working out of a sense of loyalty or a desire to go above and beyond for a leader or team. They aren't invested in the organization or in the mission. Instead, they're just trying to make it through each day and collect their paycheck. Chances are, they've already got one foot out the door, searching for greener pastures.

Now, we could dig into why some bosses end up creating this kind of atmosphere, but let's focus on what really matters: why you'd want to avoid this leadership trap, and how your choices can turn things around. It's about creating a workplace where people actually want to be, not just have to be.

When leaders prioritize the personal and professional growth of their employees, they foster an environment where everyone feels valued and motivated to contribute their best. Companies with highly engaged employees experience a 41 percent decrease in absenteeism and a 24 percent improvement in turnover. By taking the time to understand who your team members are and truly investing in them you are creating a culture of trust and respect which benefits the entire organization.

Here are some practical steps you can take to help develop a culture of trust as well as understand your team members:

Schedule a consistent weekly or biweekly one-on-one meeting with each member of your team to hear about how they are doing, what ideas they have, whether they need help, if they have questions, and how you can support them. Make your chats fun, open, and transparent. Vary the format, they don't always need to be in-person or by Zoom. A phone call often goes a lot further in developing a trusted relationship as does going out for lunch or coffee.

Take the time to applaud and commemorate your team's small wins and achievements. Recognize and celebrate life events such as work anniversaries, birthdays, weddings, and other important milestones. Remember that everyone is different. You want to create a positive and supportive environment that encourages your team to feel valued and appreciated.

Learn what each of your team member's long-term career goals are. Provide opportunities for professional development that aligns with their career aspirations. Offer training such as workshops, certification programs, or mentorship that will help them develop relevant skills and leadership abilities.

As you start to develop those key relationships you will find that your team's productivity and dynamics will flourish.

The Power of Vulnerability and Honesty

"What is your why?" This was the question asked of me and several of my colleagues in a work meeting. Honestly, my immediate thought was a paycheck. As I watched others go around the table and share their 'why' I felt like I was watching a show. Everyone seemed to have a phenomenal reason for working at our organization. The answers felt forced and disingenuous, however, one person shared that they loved their job. It was said with complete sincerity. I would have loved to be able to say I love my job, but that was not my truth. I also wanted to feel secure enough to be honest and say that my 'why' was a paycheck. Instead, I rambled. I didn't feel safe among my colleagues.

That lack of trust didn't happen overnight, it was built over the course of several years and of working in what could be described as a toxic work environment. My inability to show up as my authentic self and share my truth would have required me to be vulnerable and to model the behavior I would have liked to see from others, free of judgment or retaliation. Sometimes showing up can be scary. And sometimes it can just be exhausting.

If I publicly acknowledged that my 'why' was just a paycheck, I would be admitting that I was not invested in the organization or its mission. At that moment, I decided to give up on honesty. Privately, I had to recognize that it was time for a change.

After the meeting I gave myself the grace and space to reflect on my feelings. When I was next in that team meeting, I disclosed publicly how I felt in our last meeting regarding being asked to share our 'why'. I was proud of myself for speaking up and owning my truth. Did I do that for my colleagues, my team, or myself? I can say with no shame that it was for me.

As a leader we can always model how we would want to be treated, as well as how we would like others to show up. Positive leadership is as much for you as for your team or colleagues.   You can't control how others behave, react, or show up, but you can choose to let go when needed and not allow past behaviors to dictate how you engage.

Here are a few steps you can take to help you learn to let go:
- Take time for self-reflection, asking how you can improve your leadership style and interactions with team members. Acknowledge your part in a situation.
- Find a trusted mentor to help you navigate challenging situations. You don't have to do this by yourself.
- Don't be afraid to set boundaries and communicate them.
- Continue to lead with empathy, respect, and

professionalism. Modeling the behavior you want to see in others is extremely important.

- If your colleagues are open to a productive dialogue, talk to them.
- Practice forgiveness. Holding on to resentment hinders your growth. Forgiveness allows you to heal, improve relationships, and focus on positive outcomes.

Demonstrating vulnerability and humility as a leader, bridges gaps and builds stronger, more authentic connections within your team. Employees have reported feeling 92 percent more motivated and productive when leaders show empathy. By embodying these principles, you can lay the foundation for a supportive, productive, and resilient work environment.

Building Trust and Empathy

Working in an environment where fear is the motivator results in your staff not showing up as their best selves. What happens when staff are discouraged from sharing concerns or dissenting opinions because of fear of retaliation? Creativity, solutions, and innovation are often impacted. Leaders should want employees to perform at their best because that benefits the mission, the financials, your external partners, staff, and ultimately, you. In a company with a strong culture of trust and engagement, employees outperform their peers by nearly three times in terms of financial returns.

THE NEW C-SUITE   188

Unfortunately, there are bad leaders. They may have unresolved hurts, ulterior motives, or have simply had bad role models. This is why how you choose to lead, regardless of your title, is of paramount importance.

I have worked with several female executives who have modeled their leadership style after the male executives they encountered early in their careers. One of my former bosses, who I will call Tania, shared with me that she had noticed that these men were often ruthless and demanding, but they managed to climb the corporate ladder. Believing that adopting the same harsh approach was necessary for success, Tania became just as tough and unyielding. Over the years she advanced in her career, achieving significant professional milestones. However, while she gained some respect, feedback from many of her staff had indicated to me that she had missed an opportunity to create a more impactful legacy by leading with empathy and respect rather than replicating the negative traits she had observed. Tania built an organization that empowered others to mirror her behavior. This resulted in a toxic work environment characterized by high turnover and emotional distress among employees.

Building trust and empathy in leadership starts by creating an open and inclusive environment in which team members feel safe to express ideas and concerns. As leaders, we must encourage transparent communication and actively listen to our employees, validating their experiences and perspectives. Fostering a culture of mutual respect is possible when we recognize and appreciate the unique contributions of each team member. When mistakes happen, approach them as learning opportunities rather than occasions for punishment.

We can't always control who our leaders are, but we can challenge ourselves to show up, now or in the future, authentically and from a place of empowerment. So how do we do this?

Give yourself the time and space to reflect on what you value in a leader. Make a list of the qualities you admire in leaders. Think about leaders who have inspired you and identify the traits that they possess.

Ask yourself the tough questions. Reflect on how you show up at work. Consider questions such as:

- Do I communicate effectively with my team?
- Am I approachable and supportive?
- How do I handle stress and conflict?

Take the time to examine and explore your belief systems. Consider how they influence your actions and decisions at work. Write them down.

Don't be afraid to ask for help when you need it. Reach out to trusted and respected colleagues, supervisors, friends, or mentors for advice and honest feedback. Having different perspectives helps you improve, and more importantly, enables you to successfully navigate challenges in your career.

We grow when we invest in ourselves, and when we are open to changing and recognizing that we may not have all the answers. Continuously look for opportunities to improve yourself by taking courses, reading books on leadership, and attending workshops.

Creating a Positive Environment

Years ago, I supervised a young man whom we will call Ben. He was smart and eager, but abrasive and in a constant state of worry. As a team leader, I would always approach a new team by learning who they are, what motivates them, and what their goals are. This means taking the time to talk to everyone in one-on-one discussions, and in group settings, to foster open communication and cohesion.

I was new to the role, and we had my first in-person team meeting. I was taking my time to chat with everyone and understand their roles as well as who they were. In the middle of our meeting Ben got up and just walked out of the room. He didn't stop to explain where he was going, to excuse himself, or to even apologize. I was surprised to say the least. As the new supervisor of everyone in the room, including Ben, my response to his exit was obviously going to be closely monitored.

Instead of getting upset and frustrated or laying down the law, I chose to prioritize asking questions and understanding motivation rather than making assumptions. As Ben was not in the room, I turned to my new team and asked, 'Does that happen often?' The team was eager to share and very excited to hear my expectations regarding our meetings and how we treat each other as a team. It is important to my leadership philosophy that we communicate with one another, be respectful, and yes, explain our actions.

Ben didn't just walk out on me; he walked out on his entire team.

Ben had left the room for what he perceived to be an important media call, and he eventually returned to the meeting. Rather than admonish him in front of the team, I asked him why he had stepped out of the room, which allowed him a chance to explain to everyone his motivations. It was important to also reiterate my expectations to the team that I expected everyone to be present during our meetings. This ensured that the team would be on the same page as to my expectations going forward. It also allowed the team to see that I would be ensuring that everyone would be held accountable to the same standards. Whether intentional or not, Ben's behavior sent a message that he did not value his team, making it clear that they were not a high priority for him. This became a teachable moment. I could not expect Ben to be held to a standard that hadn't been articulated to him yet, and as noted earlier, the leadership styles we observe in others are often learned behaviors.

I saved my full list of expectations for when I met with Ben one-on-one. Ben was my second in command, and my thought-partner, and as such I wanted to help him grow as a leader and avoid belittling or embarrassing him in front of the team. This incident gave me an opportunity to illustrate to my junior team members how to be an effective leader. I modeled the behavior that I would want to see each of them demonstrate as leaders. Research by the Center for Creative Leadership indicates that when leaders demonstrate behaviors they want to see in their team members it fosters a culture of respect and trust.

You have a choice: to be a leader who cares, invests in their team, and operates as a servant leader, or, to lead with fear, intimidation, or the authority of your title. As we saw earlier, the outcome of each approach has lasting repercussions and can either build healthy teams and leaders or result in negative sentiment and higher staff turnover.

Ben and I had the conversation during our one-on-one meeting where I was able to set my expectations, and he was able to ask questions and share feedback that he had. Creating a two-way dialogue gave him a safe space to share and be heard. Over the course of our time working together, we had many conversations that ultimately built a team characterized by respect, loyalty, and unity. We understood that kindness in leadership is not a sign of weakness, but rather a way to lead with trust and respect.

How can you lead with trust and respect?

- Create a safe environment where team members feel comfortable sharing ideas, taking risks, and disagreeing without fear of retaliation or negative consequences. This encourages open dialogues, creativity, and innovation.
- Be transparent, honest, admit mistakes, and share information openly with your team. Share your own challenges and learning experiences. This humanizes you and shows that you trust your team.
- Stand by your team by supporting them even when they make mistakes or face challenges. This builds loyalty.
- Empower team members to make decisions and delegate responsibilities. This shows that you respect their judgment and trust their abilities.
- Lead by example and model the behavior you expect from your team. Be consistent in your actions. The goal is to build trust and respect over time.

Navigating Leadership with Authenticity

It's not your job to make people like or accept you; nor is it your assignment to make everyone comfortable with you. True leadership isn't about seeking approval or conforming to others' expectations. It's about standing firm in your values and principles, even when it's uncomfortable. According to the Journal of Business Ethics, leaders who consistently act with integrity and authenticity have teams with 26 percent higher productivity and 32 percent greater retention rates. When you prioritize your core beliefs and lead with authenticity, you may not please everyone, but you will build a team that respects you.

You have a choice in how you lead—whether it's with fear and intimidation, or with trust and respect. Your leadership can either build healthy teams and leaders or lead to negative emotions and turnover. By leading with a desire to see others succeed, you will create teams that flourish, are committed to the organization, and produce exceptional results.

Authentic leadership is not about authority or titles, but about transparency and vulnerability. It's about being a beacon of light, guiding your team safely through challenges and uncertainties. When you lead with empathy, trust, and respect, you build a foundation that not only motivates your team but also leaves a lasting, positive impact on their careers and lives. When leaders model these behaviors, they empower others to do the same, nurturing a supportive environment in which open communication thrives.

Leadership Lessons

You don't have to compromise your values or principles to be in a leadership role. When you lead with a desire to see others succeed, and when you listen and learn, you will build teams that flourish, produce deliverables that go above and beyond, and are always willing to step up when there is an emergency or last-minute request. You also minimize turnover, and typically create teams committed to the organization, mission, and work.

I have worked in the non-profit and public sectors for most of my career, and while having an important mission or goal to guide and lead the work can be fulfilling and help motivate a team, if leadership does not embody the values internally that they promote externally, it can create a very demoralizing environment.

Working for a mission-driven organization, and being passionate about the work, will not alone motivate teams to do their best. The mission gets the employee on board, but it doesn't replace having leaders, mentors, or colleagues that inspire each other and are genuinely committed to seeing their teams succeed.

Building a foundation of trust and empathy with your team does not just motivate them in the moment, but over the course of their careers. To this day, I am a mentor for several of my former direct reports. They come to me for career advice, for recommendations, to share exciting news, or simply to have me listen. In building that firm foundation, I have not only helped cultivate future leaders, but I have developed lasting friendships that challenge me and help me continue to grow as a leader.

Here are three action steps you can immediately implement to embrace a Civil Leadership Model:

Cultivate Empathy and Active Listening: Schedule regular one-on-one meetings with team members to understand their needs, ideas, and challenges. Your team will feel heard and valued, boosting engagement.

Provide Support and Mentorship: Ensure that team members receive the necessary guidance and resources for their tasks. Offer mentorship programs to support professional growth. This will reduce turnover and create loyalty and a long-term commitment from your team.

Lead by Example: Model the behaviors you wish to see in your team. By doing this you will build the trust, respect, collaboration, loyalty, and productivity that you desire from your employees.

These steps create a supportive, engaged, and high-performing team. When there is genuine trust there is also the ability to share hard feedback and opportunities for growth. That conversation doesn't have to be one-sided. When we see the value in asking, 'How can I do better?' or 'How can I help you?', we are further building a strong foundation that empowers employees and fosters coaching and empathy. Trust is built when we are willing to be vulnerable and to ask ourselves tough questions.

The biggest compliment I can possibly receive is knowing that my former team members see their leadership role as an opportunity to mentor and grow their direct reports. Cultivating future leaders who put people first is how we will transform the workplace.

About Paula Valle Castañon

Strategic Communications and Marketing Expert

Meet Paula Valle Castañon, a seasoned communications and marketing expert with two decades of experience across the non-profit, government, and corporate sectors.

Paula is a results-driven strategist who excels in building teams, forging strategic partnerships, and creating impactful networks.

Storytelling is at the heart of Paula's work. Whether through visual media, writing, or experiential campaigns, she is passionate about empowering others by giving them a voice. She collaborates with forward-thinking organizations and leaders to authentically tell their stories, create social value, and foster positive engagement with employees, stakeholders, and the community.

Paula's career began in journalism over 20 years ago before transitioning into communications. She holds an M.S. in Journalism from Columbia University, an M.A. in Media Studies from Sussex University (UK), and a B.A. in English Literature from the University of California at Berkeley.

Paula's dedication to storytelling and community empowerment makes her a standout leader in her field, continuously inspiring those she works with.

Holistic Leadership

By Mark Maes

With over 40 years in the business world as a Founder, Investor, CEO, and Executive Business Advisor, I have been inside hundreds, if not thousands, of businesses. Throughout that time of leading, supporting, learning, and understanding business—including the ownership, executive roles, leadership, teams, and people—has given me a profound perspective on what it takes to succeed.

You are likely aware that the key elements of effective business management are planning, leadership, people, performance, and resources. However, civil leadership emphasizes that people are at the heart of these pillars. People often forget this essential truth. Especially with the constant rate of change, noise and uncertainty. In this chapter, I aim to share the key fundamentals of business— what they are, how they work, and why they are essential to success in business, family, life, legacy, and purpose.

High Five Priority Business Mapping™, also known as H5™, is a framework that we created that builds on five critical departments: growth, marketing, sales, finance, and operations. This structured approach ensures a holistic view of the business, helping leaders drive sustainable success. Through the H5™ methods and processes, we focus on aligning business resources and efforts around core strengths, empowering people, and optimizing performance.

The H5™ principles will help you understand how to build a robust and resilient business structure, focusing on intentional behavior and measurable outcomes. I also want to ensure that it is simple, fun, light, and easy, yet super informative. So, let's dig in and keep it real.

Throughout this chapter, you will reconsider the fundamental core values required for success in business through a holistic approach. Remember, people buy from people, and business is about relationships. I believe it's crucial for your business success to maintain the clarity and truth of why you went into business. Communicate and empower the mission, vision, and values that you started with. It's important to empower your people and teams with the resources necessary to achieve objectives and reach their highest potential while filtering through the collective truth and considerations.

It is my firm belief that clarity in your mission and vision, coupled with empowering your teams, is the foundation of sustainable business success. By staying true to your initial values and purpose, you create a solid groundwork for long-term growth and resilience.

Business, Success, Happiness, Profitability, and Legacy

From my experience working with leaders, I have observed that the five big measurable goals are business, success, happiness, profitability, and legacy, which leaders often think about as lifetime goals. My question to you is, how often do you think of these? What percentage of time would you spread across them?

What if you were to realize that you have all that you need to accomplish all that you desire? How would it change your approach? While leaders often understand this concept, they commonly find it challenging to implement.

What is a belief system?

Our belief system is a complex network of ideas and principles that shape how we perceive the world and respond to various situations. Our upbringing, culture, education, and personal experiences often influence this network.

To effectively lead and inspire others, civil leaders must examine and understand their belief systems. This involves introspection and a willingness to challenge assumptions. Leaders benefit from engaging in reflective journaling, seeking feedback from trusted colleagues, and participating in professional coaching. By doing so, they can identify beliefs that may limit their potential and replace them with more empowering ones.

I worked with a leader who came to view failure as a necessary part of the path to success. He approached challenges with perseverance and a mindset centered on personal development. He saw setbacks as opportunities to learn and improve, rather than as insurmountable obstacles. Having a positive outlook can inspire your team to adopt a similar mindset, fostering a culture of continuous improvement and innovation.

His approach embodies the principles of Civil Leadership, which emphasizes empathy, resilience, and the ability to inspire others through example. However, his existing team was not familiar with this way of thinking and did not embrace it easily. Despite this, his positive outlook and performance were contagious. As time passed, the team started following his approach, leading to a more robust and proactive work atmosphere.

He was able to transform his team's mindset, demonstrating that leadership is not just about achieving success but also about guiding and uplifting others on their journey towards excellence.

The H5™ principles accomplish exactly that. Right from the beginning we establish mindset, cultures, values, and perspectives as a company standard, as well as throughout the management of each of the 5 key departments - growth, marketing, sales, finance, and operations. This holistic approach not only enhances professional skills but also cultivates a mindset that supports personal growth and leadership effectiveness.

The impact of our belief system extends beyond our professional lives. It influences our personal relationships, our health, and our overall well-being.

Subconscious Beliefs and Behavior

Subconscious beliefs operate below the level of conscious awareness and have a profound impact on our behavior. Often established in early childhood, and influenced by repeated experiences, these beliefs can persist throughout life (McLeod, 2020). Research shows that childhood experiences, such as frequent criticism, can shape long-term beliefs about self-worth and competence. Children who experience frequent criticism may develop subconscious beliefs of inadequacy, which can manifest in self-sabotaging behaviors during adulthood.

In the business world, subconscious beliefs can manifest in various ways. While working with a large construction company last year, we encountered a leader who had a deep-seated fear of failure stemming from a previous project at his last employer. He had driven some key decisions that ended badly, which caused him to avoid taking risks, even when those risks were necessary for growth. The co-manager, who was a trusted friend that had helped him secure the job, recognized the impact of this experience. He asked if that past failure could be influencing his current subconscious beliefs and behaviors. Because the leader had established trust, they were receptive to genuinely listening to this perspective.

Through further discussion, the leader could share his thoughts and assumptions. With constructive feedback and truthful insights from his co-manager, he realigned with his own abilities and regained his confidence. This process not only facilitated his internal growth, but also helped him develop as a new team member and leader.

This experience underscores the essence of Civil Leadership, which emphasizes empathy, trust, and open communication. Most often, there is beauty in the ashes, or great lessons to be learned from our mistakes when we are open to listen and to ask.

There are several approaches to uncover and address subconscious beliefs. Leaders can use techniques such as prayer, mindfulness meditation, cognitive-behavioral therapy (CBT), and neuro-linguistic programming (NLP). These approaches help individuals become aware of their thought patterns and develop healthier, more constructive beliefs.

It's crucial for the team, managers, and leaders to identify what their perfect outcome looks like, or as H5™ calls it, WPLL (What Perfect Looks Like). Identifying this from the beginning is vital for intentionality. Many managers and leaders feel incomplete or unsatisfied because they don't start by clearly defining the objectives from the outset. That's why measurable goals are so important.

People want to succeed, but they rarely know how. When you identify what perfect looks like from the beginning, you increase the likelihood of accomplishing those objectives by 70%.

An empowering resource is called the DISC test. This is a behavioral assessment tool that categorizes individuals into four main personality types - Dominance, Influence, Steadiness, and Conscientiousness - to help understand communication styles and work preferences. Watching our clients understand the logic of their personalities and characteristics is truly enlightening. Once they understand these aspects, they become much more empowered to manage them effectively, unlocking a higher level of potential by fully understanding their capabilities.

By recognizing subconscious beliefs as just that—subconscious beliefs rather than objective truths—individuals are able to begin to challenge and replace them with more empowering beliefs, such as,

"I am capable and resourceful." This shift in mindset can have a profound impact on their ability to set and achieve their goals, ultimately leading to greater satisfaction and success.

When leaders apply H5™ principles, methodologies, and protocols, they empower themselves, their people, and their teams to make sound decisions based on company values and core principles.

First, they need to actively identify and document the values by conducting workshops and brainstorming sessions with key stakeholders to define and articulate the core values of the company.

Following this, they can create value statements clearly and succinctly outlining core principles.

Educating team members about the significance of these values is the next crucial step. Developing training programs and onboarding sessions that include real-life examples and case studies help illustrate how these values guide decision-making.

Ingraining values into the organizational culture is crucial, and we can accomplish this by having regular team meetings and company-wide communications that emphasize their importance.

Celebrating and recognizing employees who exemplify these values in their work further strengthens this integration. Leaders must ensure that all major decisions align with the company's mission and strategic objectives. Developing decision-making protocols is necessary to require consideration of how actions align with core values and long-term goals.

Creating accountability structures is another vital aspect. Establishing clear metrics and KPIs (Key Performance Indicators) to measure alignment with values and principles, along with implementing feedback loops where employees can report on how values are being upheld and suggest improvements, ensures continuous alignment. Facilitating open communication by encouraging dialogue about the company's values and how they influence day-to-day operations is important. Providing platforms such as internal forums or town hall meetings where employees can share their perspectives and experiences related to company values enhances this process.

By taking these actions, leaders create a robust framework that supports alignment with the company's overarching mission and strategic goals. Leaders can create a robust framework that actively lives and reinforces values within the organization, ensuring that they are not just words on paper.

Applying Insights to Your Real-Life Experiences

Understanding and addressing our subconscious beliefs is just the beginning. The real transformation happens when we apply these insights to our daily lives. This means consciously aligning our actions with our new, empowering beliefs. We consistently work with businesses, owners, and leaders where the greatest opportunities and challenges lie in the mindset of the people and their belief systems. Many people widely accept that leaders can take incremental steps to challenge their belief that they are not effective at public speaking. By starting with brief talks in front of a mirror and then progressing to speaking in front of small, supportive groups, they can gradually build confidence and experience. Consistently applying the new belief that improvement comes with practice will probably lead to significant enhancement in public speaking skills.

In a business context, applying new beliefs might involve setting more ambitious goals, taking calculated risks, and fostering a culture of innovation and collaboration. By establishing clear standards and embracing principles, you remove uncertainties and foster an environment in which everyone understands and works towards common goals.

As standard operational procedures inclusive of intentional behavior, users start all projects, topics, or approaches with the WPLL mindset. Identifying and documenting expectations empowers the chance of success by 70-80%. By creating project success plans and personal action plans, users can guide their efforts, apply measurable goals, and set progress timelines to align with their thoughts and behaviors.

Like most habit-forming training curriculums, repetition, correct implementation, and rewards lead to the formation of new habits, with proper application and training reinforcing those new beliefs. These plans might include specific, measurable, achievable, relevant, and time-bound (SMART) goals, along with strategies for overcoming potential obstacles. By regularly reviewing and adjusting these plans, leaders can stay on track and make continuous progress towards their desired outcomes.

By taking a proactive approach rooted in the principles of Civil Leadership, we not only reinforce new beliefs but also ensure continuous growth and development within the organization. By prioritizing intentional behavior and continuous improvement, leaders and their teams foster an environment that achieves remarkable success and creates lasting positive change.

Understanding Your Potential

Every individual has immense potential; realizing it requires self-awareness and a commitment to personal growth. Understanding your potential means recognizing your strengths, weaknesses, passions, and values. It involves continuous learning and adapting to new challenges.

Leaders who understand their potential better inspire and motivate their teams. They create environments where employees feel valued and empowered to contribute their best. This not only enhances individual performance but also drives collective success and innovation within the organization.

Self-assessment tools, such as personality tests, strength assessments, and 360-degree feedback can provide valuable insights into one's potential. These tools help leaders understand their natural inclinations, areas for improvement, and how others perceive their strengths and weaknesses.

Leaders who learn through a strength assessment that they have a natural talent for strategic thinking can focus on honing this skill. The DISC and Myers-Briggs type indicators are powerful resources used to identify and empower development. Leaders also actively take part in strategic planning sessions within their organization. By leveraging their strengths, they have the ability to contribute more effectively to their team's success.

Understanding potential is not a one-time event, it's a continuous journey. As individuals grow and develop, their potential expands. Leaders should regularly reassess their skills, interests, and goals to ensure they are continually moving towards their highest potential. This ongoing process of self-discovery and growth is crucial for long-term success and fulfillment.

I encourage you to adopt the H5™ standards. Your company needs to establish clear expectations and guidelines, along with those of each of the other departments. These standards provide a framework that supports leaders in aligning their actions with the organization's mission and values, fostering a culture of excellence and achievement across the board.

Empowering Your Potential

Empowering your potential is about taking deliberate actions to unlock and maximize your capabilities. This involves setting clear goals, seeking feedback, and investing in personal and professional development. It also means surrounding yourself with mentors, coaches, and supportive networks that challenge and encourage you.

In a business setting, empowering your potential translates to fostering a culture of continuous improvement. At H5™, we advocate for this through our online learning platform, H5 LMS™. We encourage employees to take ownership of their growth and provide opportunities for skill development through courses.

One effective way to empower potential is through mentorship programs. These programs pair less experienced employees with seasoned professionals who provide guidance, support, and valuable insights. Mentorship helps individuals navigate their career paths, develop new skills, and build confidence.

Leaders can empower their teams by promoting a culture of learning. This involves providing access to training resources, encouraging knowledge sharing across our platform, and supporting employees in pursuing further education. When we value and support individuals' development, they are more likely to be engaged and motivated to contribute their best.

Marlin Machine Products, a business that provides quality custom CNC machining services for all industries, is another success story that adopted the H5™ method. Initially, the leaders had solely relied on their previous business experiences and had no formal business education. Like many sole proprietors, they sensed there was a better way but didn't know what it was. The owner, Mr. Tellez, and I connected while I was teaching and conducting the H5™ Business method training at Jack Brown University. He was open to learning and growing, making significant efforts to implement what he learned. This openness and willingness to embrace new ideas changed his life, the lives of his employees, and his business.

This story highlights the essence of Civil Leadership, where leaders prioritize learning, development, and empowerment. Success is not inherently difficult; what is challenging is not knowing the path to achieve it. By fostering a culture of continuous learning and growth, leaders are able to create an engaged, motivated, and successful team.

Empowerment involves creating opportunities for employees to take on new challenges and responsibilities. This could include assigning stretch projects, offering leadership development programs, and providing pathways for career advancement. By giving employees the chance to grow and excel, leaders can unlock their full potential and drive organizational success.

It's All About the People, Relationships, and Service with Product and Promise

Mission, Vision, and Values

The mission, vision, and values of an organization define its purpose, direction, and principles. This provides a framework for decision-making and guides the behavior of employees. A clear and compelling mission inspires and motivates the team, while a shared vision aligns everyone toward common goals.

Values represent the core beliefs and ethical standards of the organization. They shape the company culture and influence how employees interact with each other, customers, and stakeholders. Leaders must communicate and embody these values, ensuring that they become an integral part of every aspect of the business.

Our client, TGC Supply, a premier manufacturer specializing in case-goods & soft-seating products for the hospitality industry, implemented a mission, vision, and values statement for their company:

MISSION: To provide our customers with a dedicated and experienced team offering an extensive range of customized quality products at factory-direct prices with the shortest lead times in the industry.

VISION: To become the industry leader in quality, service, lead times, and pricing for hospitality product supply around the globe.

VALUES: Building relationships while providing premium products and services at competitive pricing based on our company's core values of integrity, commitment, dedication, quality, and trust.

By aligning their actions with their mission, TGC Supply continues to build a strong reputation and attract customers who share their values and align their product and service needs.

A shared vision provides a sense of direction and purpose, guiding the organization towards long-term goals. It is important for leaders to regularly communicate the vision to their team, making sure that everyone understands and is committed to achieving it. This involves setting clear objectives, tracking progress, and celebrating milestones along the way.

Core Competencies

Core competencies are the special strengths and abilities that make a business stand out from its competitors. These can include specialized skills, advanced technology, proprietary processes, or strong customer relationships. Identifying and developing core competencies is essential for sustaining success in a competitive market.

Leaders should focus on nurturing these competencies, investing in training and development, and leveraging them to create value for customers. By aligning the organization's resources and efforts around the business's core strengths, businesses can differentiate themselves and achieve long-term success.

Developing core competencies involves identifying the areas in which the company excels and build on those strengths. This could involve hiring and training employees with specialized skills, investing in technology and infrastructure, and continuously improving processes. Businesses are able to achieve long-term success by concentrating on their strengths and establishing a sustainable competitive advantage.

Corona Chamber of Commerce in Southern California—a leading chamber recognized nationwide—have strategically empowered their mission, vision, and values to set benchmarks for local businesses. Their success in fostering local business growth and community engagement exemplifies the transformative impact of identifying and leveraging core competencies. Through empowerment processes, robust communication strategies, and measurable outcomes, they have established themselves as a model of effective business development and community impact.

Core Behaviors

Core behaviors are the actions and attitudes that reflect the organization's values and contribute to its success. These include integrity, accountability, collaboration, and innovation. Core behaviors shape the company culture and influence how employees perform their roles and interact with others.

Leaders must model these behaviors and create an environment that encourages and rewards them. This involves setting clear expectations, providing regular feedback, and recognizing and celebrating positive behaviors. By fostering a culture of excellence, businesses can enhance employee engagement, performance, and satisfaction.

A company valuing integrity might implement strict ethical standards and ensure that employees are aware of and adhere to these standards. This could involve providing training on ethical decision-making, creating a whistleblower policy, and holding employees accountable for their actions.

Accountability is another important core behavior. Leaders should set clear expectations for performance and hold employees accountable for meeting those expectations. This involves providing regular feedback, recognizing achievements, and addressing performance issues promptly and fairly.

Collaboration is critical for success. Leaders should create a culture that encourages teamwork and open communication. This involves providing opportunities for employees to work together on projects, promoting cross-functional collaboration, and recognizing and celebrating team achievements.

An exemplary case illustrating the profound benefits of aligned core values and behaviors is BergmanKPRS, a company providing full-service construction, construction management, and program management services nationwide. Over the years, they have consistently understood, developed, and empowered their company through economic fluctuations, client management intricacies, and project dynamics. From team members to every individual involved, their people, managers, and leaders have embraced and applied core values and behaviors, yielding significant strength, advantages, and sustainability. They demonstrate the best ways to identify and promote important values and behaviors, showing a strong commitment to doing their best.

Communication

Effective communication is vital for organizational success. Effective communication ensures smooth information flow, well-informed decisions, and the alignment of everyone with the company's goals and strategies. This involves establishing clear communication platforms, processes, and measurables.

Leaders should implement communication channels that facilitate transparent dialogue, such as regular meetings, intranets, and collaboration tools. Processes need to be in place to ensure timely and accurate information sharing, while measurables help track the effectiveness of communication efforts. A strong communication culture fosters trust, collaboration, and innovation.

The Advantage Corporation is a great example of the benefits of structured regular team meetings. These meetings provide a culture and platform for employees to share updates, discuss challenges, and collaborate on solutions. Intranets and collaboration tools facilitate information sharing, and enable employees to work together effectively, regardless of their location.

The H5™ meeting structure, processes, and protocols create the space, mindsets, and forward-thinking approaches necessary to empower individuals in their own diversity, equity, and inclusion. By harnessing the collective synergy of individuals, we can build great teams and unlock the potential of each person.

This approach stems from the principles of Civil Leadership - leaders prioritize open communication, inclusivity, and collaboration. By fostering an environment where every team member feels valued and heard, leaders drive continuous improvement and achieve remarkable outcomes.

Measuring the effectiveness of communication efforts is important. Conducting employee surveys, tracking engagement metrics, and monitoring the impact of communication on business outcomes are some suggestions to achieve this. Leaders ensure that their team is informed, engaged, and aligned with the company's goals by continuously evaluating and improving communication strategies.

Communication platforms, processes, and metrics serve as powerful tools for broadcasting and cultivating culture within teams and organizations. H5™ methods and processes recognize these elements as crucial components of the recipe for success. Making meaningful connections within an organization is incredibly rewarding and unleashes the potential of individuals and teams alike.

Listen, Understand, Ask, Collaborate, Empower with Support

Leaders prioritize listening to their employees, customers, and stakeholders to grasp their needs and perspectives. This involves asking insightful questions, actively seeking feedback, and embracing new ideas. Studies show that people aspire to succeed, yet often lack the guidance to do so—a weakness that we aim to transform into a strength. A passionate workforce is arguably a company's greatest asset.

Collaboration and empowerment are pivotal in cultivating high-performing teams. Leaders should champion teamwork, provide necessary resources and support, and empower employees to take ownership of their roles. By nurturing a culture in which collaboration and empowerment thrive, businesses stimulate innovation, boost employee satisfaction, and achieve superior outcomes.

A company valuing collaboration might form cross-functional teams to tackle strategic initiatives. These teams unite individuals with diverse skills and viewpoints, enabling them to devise innovative solutions to complex challenges. Effective leadership ensures these teams receive the backing and resources needed for success.

Empowerment entails granting employees autonomy and accountability to show initiative, decide, and take action. This demands trust in their capabilities and provides adequate support and resources. Leaders empower teams by setting clear expectations, offering continual feedback, and recognizing achievements through celebration.

Business, Structure, Processes, and Performance - The H5™ Methods of Business

Growth and Brand Management

Growth and brand management are essential for long-term success. Growth involves expanding the business's reach, increasing market share, and exploring new opportunities. Brand management is about creating and maintaining a positive image of the company in the minds of consumers.

Effective growth and brand management requires a clear vision, strategic planning, and consistent execution. It is imperative for leaders to understand their market, identify growth opportunities, and align their brand message with customer expectations. This involves not only marketing efforts but also delivering on the brand promise through quality products and services.

A tech company looking to expand its market presence might discover an emerging market for a new type of software. By conducting thorough market research, such as analyzing customer feedback and industry trends, the company can gain insights into the needs and preferences of this market segment. Using these insights, they are able to develop a tailored product addressing specific pain points and provide unique solutions. Simultaneously, they can craft a compelling brand message emphasizing distinctive features and benefits of their software, effectively positioning it apart from competitors in the marketplace.

While I was working with a construction company, executives increased their sales by 175% and increased profitability by 23%. This was achieved by simply understanding the numbers and adjusting a couple of service lines, while aligning, rebranding, and focusing on client-centered marketing.

Brand management involves monitoring and responding to customer feedback. By actively listening to customers and making improvements based on their input, companies build trust and loyalty. This supports long-term growth; satisfied customers are likely to recommend the brand to others.

So often small businesses miss the great power and benefit of brand management. Many small businesses often neglect the potential of their company's website, which typically serves as the number one source of marketing. Don't let that be you. By actively improving your brand's online presence, and engaging with customers, you are able to affect your growth and how the market perceives you.

Marketing and Its Importance and Purpose

Marketing is the engine that drives business growth. It requires understanding what customers want, creating offers that solve problems, and effectively communicating the solutions to the right audience. The purpose of marketing is to attract, keep, and engage customers, ultimately driving sales and profitability.

Effective marketing strategies are based on thorough market research and data analysis. This involves a mix of traditional and digital channels, tailored to reach and resonate with the target audience. Leaders must stay abreast of market trends, technological advancements, and consumer behavior to ensure their marketing efforts remain relevant and impactful.

Identify targets and create dashboards to capture and manage the data and analytics. This approach helps maintain alignment and manage the plan's success, ensuring that "what gets measured gets improved."

Marketing is not just about promoting products; it's also about building relationships with customers. This involves creating personalized experiences, engaging with customers on social media, and providing exceptional customer service. By fostering strong relationships, businesses can increase customer loyalty and lifetime value.

Establishing the brand stamp or logo from the beginning is critically important as a core element in Phase 1 of the H5™ setup processes, along with other fundamentals necessary for forging success, growth, profitability, and long-term sustainability.

Sales: Converting Sales from Opportunities

Sales are the lifeblood of any business. Converting opportunities into closed-won sales requires a deep understanding of customer needs, effective communication, and strong relationship-building skills. The sales process should prioritize the needs of the customer, focusing on providing solutions rather than simply promoting products.

A successful sales strategy involves setting clear targets, tracking performance, and continuously refining techniques based on feedback and results. Training and development of the sales team are crucial to equip them with the skills and knowledge. Leveraging technology and data analytics can enhance sales efficiency and effectiveness.

For example, a company might implement a customer relationship management (CRM) system to track interactions with prospects and customers. This system provides valuable insights into customer preferences, purchase history, and pain or gain points. Sales representatives are then able to use this information to tailor their approach, addressing specific needs and building stronger relationships.

Many small businesses do not use an effective CRM. Often, this is because they haven't heard of it or have never used one. The benefits of CRM are vast, offering ease and efficiency in managing contacts and data. By selecting the appropriate CRM that is tailored to your industry and business needs, you can streamline operations from the beginning. This ensures that you keep contacts and data clean and complete.

Sales training should focus on developing key skills, such as active listening, effective questioning, and objection handling. Role-playing scenarios can help sales representatives practice these skills and gain confidence. By investing in continuous training and development, companies ensure their sales teams are well-equipped to convert opportunities into sales.

Sales success often depends on building trust and rapport with customers. This involves understanding their unique challenges, and showing how your product or service can address those challenges. Sales representatives who take the time to build genuine relationships and foster a consultative communication style with their customers are more likely to convert opportunities into sales.

Finance and Administration: The Vault and Backbone of a Business

Finance and administration form the backbone of any business, providing essential support and resources to achieve organizational goals. This includes budgeting, financial planning, accounting, and administrative functions that ensure smooth operations.

Effective financial management involves accurate forecasting, prudent expenditure, and maintaining healthy cash flow. It requires robust internal controls, and compliance with legal and regulatory requirements. Leaders must have a firm grasp of financial principles and work closely with their finance teams to make informed decisions that support business sustainability and growth.

A company that's planning to expand must conduct a thorough financial analysis to determine the feasibility of any project. This analysis considers factors such as projected revenue, expenses, and return on investment. By carefully evaluating the financial implications, leaders are able to make informed decisions that support long-term growth.

Many of our clients compliment and comment on the benefits and added value of deliberate behavior in financial planning and administration.

Administrative functions, such as human resources and office management, are critical for business success. These functions ensure that the organization operates smoothly and efficiently, providing support for employees to perform their roles effectively. Leaders should prioritize building strong administrative teams and systems to support the overall success of the business.

Many of our clients in the small business division show up without an accounting system in place; many are using spreadsheets. We see this as a significant opportunity rather than a fault. By introducing structured financial systems and processes through our H5™ method, businesses are empowered to transform their operations and achieve greater efficiency and growth.

Operations: Providing What Was Sold Under a Fixed Budget, and Outperforming Expectations for Quality

Operations are where the business delivers on its promises. This involves managing the production and delivery of goods and services within a fixed budget while maintaining high standards of quality. Effective operations management ensures that the business meets customer expectations and operates efficiently.

Key aspects of operations management include process optimization, supply chain management, and quality control. Leaders must focus on continuous improvement, leveraging technology and innovation to enhance operational efficiency. By exceeding customer expectations, and delivering consistent quality, businesses build a strong reputation and drive repeat business.

By continuously analyzing and improving their processes, businesses can increase efficiency, reduce costs, and improve product quality. By working closely with suppliers, and maintaining strong relationships, companies ensure a reliable supply of materials and components. These processes help businesses identify the best processes and measurables specific to each business and its conditions and needs.

Quality control is a critical aspect of operations management. This involves implementing rigorous testing and inspection procedures to ensure that products meet or exceed customer expectations. By maintaining high standards of quality, businesses build trust and loyalty with their customers, supporting long-term success.

Conclusion

Adopting a holistic approach to business entails addressing all facets of the organization beyond mere financial outcomes. Leaders must prioritize fundamental aspects, such as belief systems, subconscious behaviors, real-life experiences, potential, and empowerment. Using H5™ methods, companies optimize business structure, processes, and performance, whether they are a startup or a seasoned business with a large workforce.

H5™, aka High Five Priority Business Mapping™, ensures a positive impact on your vision, business, teams, and overall performance. Ultimately, leaders must emphasize people, relationships, and service, ensuring these align with the company's mission, vision, and values.

By embracing these principles, leaders can drive sustainable success, generate enduring value, and build a meaningful legacy. Success goes beyond financial achievements; it involves making a positive impact on people's lives, and the world. Adopt a holistic perspective, lead with purpose, and inspire with passion. Protect your joy, live our promise and be deliberate about your success.

"I can't," seldom does.

About Mark Maes

Founder & CEO, Maes and Associates

Meet Mark Maes, the Founder and CEO of Maes and Associates, a leading business consulting and management firm.

With over 40 years of experience in leadership and business strategy, Mark has built a reputation for excellence and innovation.

Before launching Maes and Associates in 2009, Mark spent over three decades at the helm of M&M Interiors, a Riverside-based company he founded. Under his leadership, M&M Interiors grew to become the fourth largest non-union C-9 contractor in California, a testament to his strategic vision and commitment to success.

Mark's expertise spans Marketing, Advertising, Construction Law, Management, and Architectural blueprint design. He's sharpened his leadership skills through engagements with Fortune 500 CEOs at T.E.C. and through executive development at BBL.

At Maes and Associates, Mark provides top-tier consulting

services to CEOs, executives, and small business owners. He's the creator of the High Five Priority Business Mapping methodology, which helps businesses crystallize their vision and implement actionable steps. He also developed H5 LMS, an online platform offering courses on business best practices.

Mark's dedication to empowering others and his vast knowledge continue to make a significant impact in the business world, guiding leaders to achieve their fullest potential.

Change Leadership

By Marina St. Cyr

What does the word 'change' evoke when you hear it? Do you sigh and want to run for cover, or do you rub your hands together and yell "Bring It On!"? Depending on your experience of change, personally or professionally, you may have a natural aversion or even excitement about the concept of change. I have been in both camps: welcoming change and avoiding it. This chapter focuses on workplace changes that are required to move people in a new direction. Whether you are the pushing or receiving side of a change initiative, you will find opportunities for reflection and consideration that require perspective adjustments in order to advance forward.

Workplace changes disrupt the norm, and can include adjustments to:

- Process/procedures

- Technology platforms
- Team members
- Management
- Ownership
- New products
- Discontinued products
- New strategies
- Or a completely new vision and company direction.

If you are expected to lead a change, you may first need to honestly evaluate your own willingness and outlook regarding the required outcomes. Self-awareness can be both necessary and painful. Knowing where you are and where you need to be will determine your effectiveness in leading others. You will need to know how you feel about change, and what makes you resist or embrace it.

How do you respond during times of discomfort and uncertainty? Leaders need to be less self-promoting and more people-promoting. There needs to be an awareness that your impact as a leader extends far beyond the bottom line. There is a spectrum of how people react to change, ranging from full resistance to full embrace. You need to be aware of where you and others fall on that spectrum.

It's important to recognize that your early life experiences may have left an imprint on your openness to change, positively or negatively. If you experienced a family breakup, this could result in resisting leadership-type changes in the workplace and feel discomfort facing the unknown. Loss and change causes anxiety. You could also have been in unsafe environments, and your need for control is threatened with changes that will potentially be imposed on you.

On the opposite side of the spectrum, a new sibling arriving on the scene could have been an experience of anticipation and joy. I, for example, attended 15 different schools before graduating high school. I come from a mixed-race family, navigating different racial neighborhoods and socio-economic environments with each of these changes. Adapting quickly was a learned survival skill, but also seemed like continuous new adventures to me. As a result, I have often found myself thriving in companies that had massive growth or frequent change, and I have volunteered with organizations that were constantly growing and adding new programs. Someone in the same situation might have had an opposite experience. They could have experienced instability, a sense of dread, anxiety, and resentment.

In studying change management for the workplace, I've learned that the psychology behind change involves emotional cycles that people go through before they can arrive at a place of acceptance.

In this chapter, I will cover practical ways to move through resistance to acceptance. Together, we will navigate recognizing and understanding resistance in yourself and in others. I will address the importance of moving ourselves and others from mere acceptance to embracing a growth-based mindset—one that believes change is the key to transformative growth. Civil leaders in today's environment deal with rapid-fire change and we must be leaders capable of navigating others through it. We must desire a unified outcome and pursue this with care and compassion. We may find that influencing others' mindset towards change is much harder than we anticipated. Changing hearts and changing mind to reach a desired end goal, could be more than we bargained for.

Embracing Change: The Imperative for Growth

The fact is, change is an inevitable, and an unavoidable component of our personal and professional lives. It is important to understand the natural stages we go through, however, understanding these stages doesn't move the needle, action does. Until you embrace change, you will not be effective in moving anyone from point A to point B. So how do we begin to 'embrace' change?

First, as a leader, understand and recognize the motivating behaviors of a negative response to change. Second, recognize your own resistance or self-limiting beliefs. Third, you will need practical and actionable steps to help mitigate chaos and uncertainty. And lastly, we will discuss mindset and how we approach and embrace the concept of change. It is change that promotes growth and transformation.

Why It Is Hard ... In All Things Gain Understanding

To many, the very mention of change evokes feelings of fear, uncertainty, and anxiety, naturally leading to resistance. I've witnessed resistance in multiple situations, and it often shows up as defensiveness, rebellion (in order to maintain control), and blocking. Unfortunately, it can also show up as revenge and sabotage. Resistance is a defensive response and coping mechanism to protect oneself from harm, discomfort, and perceived negative outcomes.

Resistance can be reduced once we first recognize it, understand it, and take practical steps to overcome it.

We need to understand that it is entirely possible that people go through emotional cycles similar to the stages of grief: denial, anger, bargaining, depression and acceptance. A model outlined by Kubler-Ross' change curve consists of seven stages: shock, denial, frustration, depression, experiment, decision, and integration. This provides a framework for understanding how individuals react to change and how they can adjust. By recognizing that there are stages to change adaptation, we systematically ensure smoother navigation when we align our knowledge with action that addresses the various stages.

Bridging the Gap

Actions that have helped me navigate teams and limit the chaos surrounding change initiative include communication, education, support, and team contribution.

Communication

Studies have shown that, on average, it takes at least five to seven repetitions of a message before it can be embraced during major changes. A message surrounding change must be concise and compelling to explain the need, the solution, and the expected impact. It is important for the language and key points to remain consistent across all communications; using multiple communication channels is important. This could include team meetings, video messages, town halls, intranet posts, one-on-ones, small groups, and company-wide written messages. The message should be tailored to different groups, especially concerning the impact on them. A communication advantage for a leader is knowing an employee's communication style and adjusting to the level of detail they need and prefer.

Leaders throughout the organization must ensure consistent messaging and be fully equipped to handle questions. All communication starts here, and it is important for the messaging to be vetted out thoroughly. Nothing will undermine a change initiative like a fragmented leadership team sending different messages and undertones about a change initiative. It is important to establish a culture of open communication channels throughout the process. The message should be reinforced continually, and feedback welcomed and discussed with leadership to ensure consistency and to allow for proper monitoring and adjusting where appropriate.

Education

The more training and resources you can provide, the better supported individuals will feel. Education provides reinforcement. Education is a tool that many companies may not want to add, especially when resources and time are a constraint. However, I've learned that well established plans and investments upfront will help people run together. Otherwise, more time is spent "pulling" people along, which hurts morale, breeds discontentment, encourages resentment, and is energy ineffectively spent. Education comes in many forms. Investing first in leadership development is crucial. Leaders must be equipped to lead and manage teams through a change process. Leadership teams need to be able to identify questions and challenges that arise once a change announcement is made. Educating leaders helps them feel equipped and confident to influence and impact their teams. Tools should be developed for recurring, consistent and frequent reference, such as infographics, presentations, emails and even a "Frequently Asked

Questions" resource. A forum to allow for role playing provides an educational platform that builds confidence and showcases a variety of approaches to various situations.

Skills training will be mandatory if processes, systems, or equipment changes are being implemented. It must be thorough, repeated, practiced, and evaluated. A basic template for skills training involves teaching the process, demonstrating it, allowing the trainee to practice the process with guidance, observing the trainee, making necessary adjustments, and having the trainee complete the process independently at least three times without support. Allowing hands-on practice is critical for success. Merely showing a process change, or using a classroom/presentation style training without any hands-on opportunities to learn has never worked well.

Support

Provide emotional support and encouragement to help individuals navigate through their feelings and challenges. Remember, everyone processes change differently. A civic-minded leader will not see this as a necessary evil but an opportunity to establish a culture of care and respect. As mental health awareness has become more prevalent, leaders must understand the importance of their employees' wellbeing. Change is traumatic for many people, and it's even harder when something that has been the norm for many years is being changed.

Providing necessary support allows employees an avenue to work though their own resistance faster. These are opportunities for mentoring and coaching and this one-on-one or small group opportunity will build a foundation of trust. Once trust is established, a team can truly run together and accomplish feats that could not be accomplished alone. High performance teams are built on trust. Collaborative teams are built on trust. Intentionally creating support avenues helps teams and companies' flourish. I've witnessed groups of people who initially dragged their feet come together and encourage one another, even without their leaders, to move initiatives forward. It is a rewarding experience for a leader who has made the investments upfront to build up their people.

Team Contribution

Involve individuals in the change process by seeking their input and feedback, this increases buy-in and ownership. It is often overlooked, but all experienced, strong leaders know that allowing those who are impacted to have a voice and contribute makes a critical difference. True leaders don't need to take the credit; they influence and empower their teams towards results. Most people want to feel like they matter and that their contribution counts. Involving people in the change process creates a sense of ownership and responsibility, which is a win-win scenario.

To effectively bridge the gap, a leader must be willing to assess their own knowledge, experience, and approach to leading. What worked in the past will not always be effective today. To manage humanely, we must be motivated to understand and address the different emotions and stages of the change curve, and we must care for people throughout the process. By doing so, individuals can gradually move towards acceptance and embrace the change positively. It is a leader's role to navigate the process in a way that supports and encourages their employees. Utilizing the tools and practices I provide here will never substitute the human need for connection and care, especially during times of great change. A leader's communication and support are critical to impacting an initiative positively or negatively. A leader forms the bridge between point A and point B.

When we are able to reframe the idea of change, not as a source of stress, but as a springboard for opportunity and growth, we begin to create an environment of "possibility". Recognizing change as a catalyst for transformation is essential for not only navigating the ever-evolving landscape of the workplace, but also for driving personal and organizational growth. As a leader, when you help others navigate a mindset change, and create environments with positive experiences of change, you have equipped people in an impactful way. This is a rewarding aspect of leadership.

Leaders are expected to drive results. Embracing change within an organization can catapult growth for the business. When done successfully, your influence as a leader rises in the eyes of stakeholders. Effective change management positively impacts your leadership reputation, and the overall company can be impacted in the following ways:

Fostering innovation and creativity: By embracing change, organizations create an environment that encourages innovative thinking and creative problem-solving. This leads to the development of new products, services, and processes that drive business growth. Leaders who champion change inspire their teams to think outside the box and explore new possibilities.

Adapting to market dynamics: Change allows businesses to stay agile and responsive to shifting consumer preferences and market trends. This adaptability enables companies to seize new opportunities, enter emerging markets, and maintain a competitive edge. Leaders who embrace change guide their organizations to pivot quickly and effectively in response to external factors.

Cultivating a growth mindset: Embracing change promotes a culture of continuous learning and improvement. This growth mindset encourages employees to take calculated risks, learn from failures, and constantly seek ways to enhance their skills and knowledge. Leaders who embody this mindset inspire their teams to embrace challenges and view them as opportunities for growth.

Enhancing organizational resilience: By regularly adapting to change, businesses become resilient and better equipped to handle unexpected disruptions. This resilience is crucial for long-term success and sustainability. Leaders who navigate change effectively build trust and credibility within their organizations.

Attracting and retaining top talent: Organizations that embrace change are more appealing to high-performing individuals who seek dynamic and innovative work environments. This helps in attracting and retaining top talent, which is essential for business growth. Leaders who create such environments enhance their influence by becoming talent magnets.

Driving technological advancement: Embracing change often involves adopting new technologies, which significantly improve efficiency, productivity, and customer experience. This technological edge leads to substantial business growth. Leaders who champion technological adoption position themselves as forward-thinking and visionary.

Fostering a culture of innovation: By consistently embracing change, leaders create a culture where innovation is celebrated, and failure is seen as a learning opportunity. This culture drives continuous improvement which leads to breakthrough ideas that fuel business growth.

Improving decision-making: Change often requires leaders to make quick, informed decisions. This hones their decision-making skills and improves their ability to navigate complex situations, further enhancing their leadership influence.

Building stronger teams: Navigating change together strengthens team bonds and improves collaboration. Leaders who guide their teams through change effectively build stronger, more cohesive units that are better equipped to drive business growth.

Embracing change within an organization not only catalyzes business growth but also significantly enhances leadership influence. It fosters innovation, improves adaptability, attracts top talent, and builds resilience. Leaders who successfully champion change position themselves and their organizations for sustained success in today's dynamic business landscape.

The Growth Mindset: The Cornerstone of Embracing Change

Carol Dweck introduced the concept of a growth mindset in her 2006 book "Mindset: The New Psychology of Success". This groundbreaking work synthesized decades of her research on human motivation and self-conceptions, which she had been studying since the early 1970s.

Dweck presented her theory of two primary mindsets - fixed and growth - and explored how these mindsets significantly impact an individual's approach to challenges, learning, and personal development. The growth mindset is based on the belief that one's abilities and intelligence can be developed through effort, learning, and persistence, rather than being fixed traits.

While the book popularized the concept for a wider audience in 2006, it's important to note that Dweck's research leading to this theory had been ongoing for many years prior. Her work bridging developmental, social, and personality psychology laid the foundation for the mindset theory. The publication of "Mindset" in 2006 marked a pivotal moment in bringing these ideas to the forefront of educational and psychological discussions, sparking widespread interest and application of growth mindset principles in various fields.

A **fixed mindset** views abilities as static and unchangeable. It is a belief system that intelligence and talents are fixed traits that cannot be developed or changed. A **growth mindset** sees potential and possibility in every situation. The word 'possibility' represents to us the idea of potential. I believe that each of us wants to live out our potential and to live in excellence. This cannot happen when we approach change from a place of resistance.

Jim Kwik's book "Limitless" offers several specific techniques to develop a growth mindset:

Flipping your mindset: Identify and challenge limiting beliefs and assumptions that hinder personal growth. This involves actively questioning negative self-talk, and reframing thoughts to be more expansive and growth oriented.

Overcoming limiting beliefs: Kwik emphasizes the importance of changing self-talk from limiting statements to more empowering ones.

Viewing mistakes as learning opportunities: Mistakes are not failures but chances to learn and improve. Kwik encourages readers to stop getting frustrated by mistakes and instead focus on how quickly they can overcome problems both practically and emotionally.

Small Simple Steps: This technique involves breaking down larger goals into smaller, manageable tasks. By focusing on small, achievable steps, readers can build momentum and confidence in their ability to grow and improve.

Emphasizing effort over innate ability: Abilities and intelligence are developed through effort and learning, which is a core principle of the growth mindset.

Cultivating a "limitless" mindset: The overall philosophy of the book encourages readers to challenge their perceived limitations and expand their notion of what's possible, fostering a mindset of continuous growth and improvement.

Practicing self-appreciation: The importance of appreciating oneself and one's efforts helps reinforce a positive, growth-oriented mindset.

Daily practice and repetition: Consistent practice is important in developing new skills and mindsets. Kwik encourages readers to engage in daily activities that reinforce a growth mindset.

By implementing these techniques, readers are encouraged to shift their perspective from fixed limitations to endless possibilities for growth and improvement, which is the essence of developing a growth mindset. By adopting a growth mindset, we can transform our perception of change from a threat to an opportunity. More importantly, when we impact the mindsets of those around us, we help them to see possibility. If we do not see change as a catalyst, and as a necessary component to growth, we will never reach a place of peak performance, personally or professionally.

So how do we actually adopt a growth mindset? First, it is easier said than done. I have adopted six key principles repeatedly. I'll share some experiences to help you relate to these:

Embrace Challenges

Rather than shying away from difficult situations, recognize them as opportunities to learn and grow. When faced with change, identify how this can positively contribute to your experience and skill sets on the other side.

When our warehousing staff was asked to transition from a handwritten process for picking and receiving orders and tracking inventory to an electronic system using scan guns, there was distrust and discomfort in adopting the new system.

The process and changes were not easy. In order to truly get the team to recognize the need for the changes, we had to show that the amount of errors and cost were associated with inventory errors, lost time, and inaccurate processing. Utilizing the scan guns would take time to learn but would eventually save time in normal transactions and eliminate errors such as shipping the wrong product. By scanning barcodes, the guns would notify you immediately if you attempted to ship a product incorrectly.

The recognition that this skill set would make each employee more productive was intriguing. However, by learning a new skill set, our employees were equipped to train on a system used by more advanced warehousing systems today. This would allow for more opportunities for our employees, even if that meant it wasn't with us.

Learn from Criticism

Constructive feedback is a valuable tool for growth; welcome feedback as a way to improve and steer your development in the right direction. This is always easier said than done, however effective feedback from a trusted source, such as a trusted superior, a mentor, or coach can identify any blind spots.

Most leaders believe they are self-aware, but surveys and research reflect statistics that alarmingly show us this is not the case.

Criticism has a negative connotation, but your willingness to listen, understand, and challenge your own thoughts could change your path. It has been the constructive criticism that I have received from trusted superiors who had my best interest in mind that helped me recognize and change those traits necessary to grow and advance in my career. Some qualities and traits I exhibited needed correcting and I'm grateful for honest and bold feedback provided from those I admire and respect.

Value Effort

Understand that effort is a vital component of success. The path to mastering new skills and adapting to new environments requires patience and persistence. Encourage yourself and others for the efforts made. Recognize that when we tackle difficult challenges, we build confidence by proving to ourselves that we can do hard things. Grit and perseverance are not as common as we think, so anyone willing to exert the extra effort to grow, change, or learn should be applauded and valued. This could mean encouraging an employee taking a class, someone going back to school, or an employee training to learn a new skill set.

Celebrate Progress

Acknowledge the progress you make, no matter how small. Celebrating milestones along the way helps maintain motivation and reinforces the belief that you are capable of growth. I didn't learn this until recently. I have been what some label an 'insecure overachiever.' As such, I continuously pushed myself, was my own worst critic, and nothing I did felt like enough. I quickly moved from one win to the next, never pausing to celebrate. When this was brought to my attention and I was asked to pause and acknowledge what I had accomplished, I realized that by not honoring myself, I was limiting myself. It created a mindset that I'd never truly be 'good enough.' I may not have believed that 100%, but my actions showed that milestones and their celebration were not important. Recognizing this, I now see celebrating milestones as a form of self-care I hadn't offered myself before. I now look for milestones and ways to celebrate along the way, even before a project is finished.

Adapt

People and companies stand out as resilient when they are able to pivot and quicky adapt to unexpected circumstances. Continually remind yourself and others that adapting well brings with it the reputation of resilience. Adapting also brings with it more opportunity. When you spend less time in resistance, adjust quickly, and embrace new circumstances, people, and visions, you can bring joy and excitement with you. Some of my greatest blessings have come from unexpected changes. New bosses, new peers, new offices, and new projects have broadened my perspective, widened my circles, and improved the way I show up.

Recognize Resistance

Resistance is akin to putting up a wall. One of the most common recognizable patterns is procrastination. As soon as we notice these patterns, we must redirect ourselves and others with a sense of urgency. If you need an accountability partner, or you need to incentivize yourself, do so. You must find ways to see and recognize these limiting patterns and crush them. Convince yourself by whatever means necessary that pushing through and pushing forward will take you places you have not yet imagined, and then believe it.

Moving from Fear to Excitement

Fear and anxiety are common reactions to change, but they do not have to govern our actions. Emotionally led leaders are ineffective and rarely respected. The same holds true for employees. We must recognize the value of rational behavior and logical reasoning to navigate the difficult situations we encounter. Inappropriate or extreme behaviors have unexpected consequences. Displaying fear and anxiety as a leader causes panic, doubt, and usually drives inaction. The inability to act is what separates most people and companies from being winners. I'm not saying you shouldn't experience fear or anxiety; I'm saying you cannot act or lead from it, and you certainly cannot freeze and avoid making decisions.

By harnessing a concept known as emotional intelligence and reframing our mindset, fear can be replaced with excitement and curiosity. These are the soft skills that are demonstrated in true leaders.

Emotional Intelligence in Change Management

In 1995, Daniel Goleman published a book called "Emotional intelligence: Why It Can Matter More Than IQ". This book explained and popularized the concept of emotional intelligence. Emotional intelligence involves self-awareness, self-regulation, motivation, empathy, and social skills. It is the ability to recognize, understand, and manage our emotions and influence the emotions of others.

The components of emotional intelligence are crucial when navigating change and are defined as follows:

Self-Awareness: Understand your emotional reactions to change. Acknowledge your fears and anxieties, but also recognize your strengths and capabilities.

Self-Regulation: Manage your emotions effectively. Practice mindfulness and stress-relief techniques to maintain composure and clarity.

Motivation: Focus on intrinsic motivators, such as personal growth and the satisfaction of overcoming challenges. Visualize the positive outcomes of change.

Empathy: Consider the feelings and perspectives of others. Support your colleagues by showing understanding and compassion for their experiences with change.

Social Skills: Foster open communication and collaboration. Build strong relationships that provide support and encouragement during times of transition.

The Role of Executive Leaders in Embracing Change

It is imperative that executive leaders not only understand the dynamics of change but also to lead by example in embracing it. As a leader, your approach to change will set the tone for the organization. Now more than ever, someone aspiring to leadership cannot excel in today's climate without believing that change has to be seen as opportunity and possibility.

We must have the willingness to showcase our own journeys in these areas. We need to personalize how change has positively impacted our lives, even when we may have first resisted it.

I credit my current CEO and Partner, Scott Duke, with a phrase he coined "disruption is our friend." He repeated this motto continuously. It became a tool to rally the troops—not to run and take cover when massive interruptions occurred, but to get excited because we knew that while others froze, we would lean in and take action. We weren't afraid to run into the storm and move with it while others ran for shelter.

During COVID, companies pivoted and sustained while competitors in the same industry crumbled. The idea that the unexpected could and should work in your favor is a mindset. The repeated use of this frame became critical when a frontline manager shared some industry news that garnered a gasp from several people as she read the news on her phone. She paused for just a moment and said, "But wait, disruption is our friend, let's think about how we should seize this opportunity". Even though these weren't my genius words, I felt proud to see that it was changing the way people in our company thought about unexpected challenges.

It is critical to decide and be convinced now on our posture towards change.

We must understand and recognize that some people will resist. It is up to us to persuade them with a vision for the possible. This excitement starts with us, and we should make it contagious. After all, disruption is our friend, and we are about to jump these hurdles together.

I've read countless books and articles on change management. When I don't know what to do, I've often looked for resources to guide me. Here is what I know: nothing teaches you like action. To build confidence and muscle in your weak areas you must exercise and practice new tools and new mindsets. I have failed in this area countless times in my personal and professional life.

What I've learned is that there are strategies I've had to embrace to lead change, first in myself, and only then was I able to help others.

Multiple changes are experienced from processes, to products, to people and to culture. These are go-to strategies for me. Today I've navigated and led multiple implementations surrounding mergers and acquisitions. These are difficult. People's lives are impacted.

I will share a difficult leadership experience that had a huge impact on me. I'll then share the strategies I learned since and have employed in multiple disciplines and change initiatives:

Several years ago, I had a painful and impactful experience, leading a team on a passion project. We were going to work with an organization that helped children impacted by trafficking in another country. This work required months of training, learning a new culture, and preparing inexperienced people to go out and work with victimized children, support experienced workers in this field, and to serve the community.

We had some unexpected changes and additions to our team at the last hour. They did not receive the training the others had, nor did they get the opportunity to bond and build trust with the team prior to navigating this venture. I thought I understood the assignment; I didn't. My plans and training didn't align with what the organization we were supporting were expecting. I was caught in an awful dilemma. We weren't meeting the needs of the organization, and I had an entire team looking to me to pivot, adjust, and keep them encouraged and motivated under strenuous circumstances. I had my organization's reputation to protect, I had the dreams and experiences of my team members in my hands, and I had the organization I loved and respected disappointed and resentful of what we brought to the table.

My leadership skills had never been tested in so many areas to this point in my life. However, I realized that I had many experiences to draw upon to make decisions, act, and move forward. I failed at the current assignment and yet I still had an opportunity to make the most out of what I was faced with.

After many tears and setbacks, and very little sleep we regrouped, adjusted our plans, and met the demands to the best of our ability. We were even met with a lawsuit and an attack on my leadership after the event. It was an incredibly challenging time.

Out of the ashes, one of my team members took a bold leap of faith, leaving the comfort of her home and business to embark on a two-year journey to become a trauma counselor for the children in this organization. In the process, I earned the respect and love of the founder of the organization we supported.

This founder has gone on to open new rescue operations in other countries and has become a very dear friend. The entire experience was challenging and uncomfortable and this woman who had worked with countless organizations pulled me aside to acknowledge that she was more than impressed with my ability to navigate the circumstances with both strength and grace.

It required acknowledging that accountability was needed from multiple parties, including her organization. As a result of this situation, we have discussed leading her organization together in the future. At the time, it was one of the hardest experiences. My team watched the attacks come my way and felt helpless. At the same time, I needed to lead them not to 'react' but to move forward in a way that honored themselves and others.

The experience was life-changing for each of us. We still had work to do and people to impact. Our perspectives were changed and challenged. It was tough, but I wouldn't change it if I could.

In this experience and in many others, the strategies I had to embrace included:

Demonstrating Resilience: I've been knocked down more times than I can count. I've become pretty good at "getting back up". The ability to be wrong, to learn from mistakes, to feel paralyzed by the unexpected, and to push forward in spite of these, is resilience. It is not staying down, it is not giving up, it is trying again. Your experiences and your stories can remind people of what is possible. Resilience is a beautiful and inspiring picture of hope and possibility.

Inspire a Shared Vision: Create a compelling vision that inspires and motivates employees. Help them see the bigger picture and how their contributions are vital to the organization's success. Employees desire to connect to the vision, to see their relevance to this future state. They want to understand how a future state or this recommended change will have a positive impact in the community, the industry, or the world.

Cultivate Trust: Build and maintain trust by being transparent, consistent, and reliable. Trust is the foundation of a successful change initiative. Trust is formed when there is clarity of vision; ambiguity here is not your friend.

Empower Others: Empower your team by delegating

responsibilities and encouraging autonomy. Provide opportunities for professional growth and development. Involving others to further shape the vision fosters a sense of ownership and commitment. Setting an intentional goal to articulate the necessity of their contribution to make a meaningful impact is important.

Lead with Empathy: Show genuine concern for the well-being of your employees. Be approachable and supportive. Take time to understand their perspectives. Being curious and willing to listen will begin to ease tension employees feel. Last, but not least, be patient.

A common leadership challenge is critical short-term deadlines. Timelines are sensitive, and we want our teams to get with the program and get with it fast. Here is the warning: rushing employees and pushing them without their buy-in will hurt the organization. You may not get 100% of the people on board, but you should aim for it. The momentum of many will be worth the wait and ensure you have a running start.

Be willing to invest in your team. Make the investment to focus on mindset. No matter the outcome of the current planned change, facilitating your team to embrace a growth mindset is beneficial both now and in the future. Leaders today generally embrace the philosophy of having impact that far exceeds what is being done. The soft skills that today's leaders embrace position them for far greater results and peak performance than those achieved by prior generations. I need my team to either be on board or leave the team.

However, rushing employees before they have buy-in will hurt your ability to execute. The investment of time to get employees on board allows them to run with you. Momentum keeps everyone running in the same direction at the same time.

Case Study: Crafting an Engaging Execution Plan

If you have ever been part of adopting a technology implementation that changes processes in every department, you will know that it is one of the hardest changes you could encounter. The investment is huge both in human and capital resources. I, with no technical background, was tasked with implementing a new ERP. I had to identify a solution and execute the implementation from beginning to end. It was challenging for me as the leader, and it was hard for all of our employees.

Implementation of a Detailed Execution Plan

Phase 1: Preparation and Communication

Leadership Commitment: The executive leaders must publicly endorse the change, demonstrating their understanding and commitment. They should emphasize the benefits and necessity of the transformation.

Transparent Communication: Clearly communicate the vision, goals, and timeline of the change. Address potential concerns and provide a platform for employees to voice their questions and feedback.

Involving Employees: Encourage employees to participate in the planning process. Form focus groups and include representatives from various departments to gather insights and build a sense of ownership.

Phase 2: Training and Support

Skills Assessment: Conduct a skills assessment to identify training needs. Provide tailored training programs that equip employees with the necessary knowledge and skills.

Mentorship Programs: Pair employees with mentors who can offer guidance and support throughout the transition. This builds confidence and reduces anxiety.

Resources and Tools: Ensure employees have access to resources and tools needed in order to succeed. Create a centralized hub for information and support.

Phase 3: Implementation and Feedback

Pilot Programs: Start with pilot programs to test the new system with a small group of users. Gather feedback and make necessary adjustments before a full-scale rollout.

Continuous Feedback Loop: Establish a continuous feedback loop where employees can share their experiences and suggest improvements. Act on this feedback to make the transition smoother.

Celebrate Milestones: Recognize and celebrate milestones and successes along the way. Acknowledge the hard work and dedication of employees.

Phase 4: Sustaining Momentum

Reinforce the Change: Continually communicate benefits and successes of the change. Share success stories and case studies that highlight positive outcomes.

Adapt and Evolve: Be open to making adjustments as needed. Change is an ongoing process; flexibility is key to sustaining momentum.

Embracing change is not just a necessity for survival in today's world; it is a pathway to growth, innovation, and lasting success. By fostering a growth mindset, leveraging emotional intelligence, and implementing a detailed execution plan, organizations can ensure change is an exciting and engaging journey for everyone involved. As an executive leader, it is your responsibility to lead the charge, embody resilience, and inspire your team to embrace the possibilities that change brings. Together, we can transform challenges into opportunities and create a dynamic, thriving workplace. This is what you were called to do.

About Marina St. Cyr

Sr. Vice President of Operations & Partner, Access Partners, Inc.

Meet Marina St. Cyr, the powerhouse Sr. Vice President of Operations and Partner at Access Partners, Inc. A talented leader, Marina oversees a diverse portfolio of companies spanning Accounting & Finance, Human Resources, Legal, Operations, and Corporate Administration. Her expertise shines in mergers and acquisitions, where she's led multidisciplinary teams to success across various business operations.

Today, Marina's influence extends to managing multiple ventures, including a sales organization, two import and wholesaling companies, a warehouse and distribution entity, and a portfolio of seven commercial properties.

Her experience in manufacturing laid the groundwork for her prowess in supply chain management, organizational strategy, and treasury management. Marina excels at leading cross-functional teams and thrives in the fast-paced, high-growth environment of entrepreneurial businesses.

Outside of her professional life, Marina is a proud wife and mother of four, with a passion for reading and exploring global culinary delights. She's also a dedicated volunteer, with over a decade of experience leading large volunteer groups on service projects across the world.

Conclusion:

Stepping off the stage at the California HR Conference in Anaheim, I was filled with a sense of déjà vu. Just moments earlier, I had delivered a keynote on Civil Leadership to a few hundred HR professionals, and now, as I walked towards the table set up for my book signing, a familiar feeling washed over me. It was the same feeling I had years ago, sitting in the front row at this very conference, listening to Patagonia's keynote.

I remember how it left me changed, inspired, and activated, and now, here I was, hoping my words had sparked the same in others.

When I arrived at the table, I was greeted by a line of people eager to get a copy of my earlier published book and share their thoughts. One after another, they expressed how much the topic resonated with them, how timely the message was, and how they appreciated the global perspective I brought to the conversation.

Their words confirmed that the message I had shared was not just relevant but urgently needed.

As I later made my way to facilitate a session on Situational Leadership, one of the conference hosts stopped me, excitement evident in his expression. He eagerly shared that the speaker who followed me, a renowned figure in his industry, had referenced my talk multiple times during his keynote, praising its relevance and accuracy.

This unsolicited validation sparked a realization within me: the message of Civil Leadership is not just timely; it's universal. It transcends generational boundaries and resonates deeply with people across all fields, touching both hearts and minds.

This experience left me more convinced than ever that Civil Leadership is a conversation we must continue, and I'm grateful to be part of this important dialogue.

As we move forward, let us carry this message with us—empowering others, leading with empathy, and driving change in ways that matter.

The journey of Civil Leadership has only just begun, and together, we can shape a future where leadership is not just about positions of power, but about the positive impact we leave behind.

Thank you for being part of this journey.

Warm regards,
Tiana Sanchez

Notes

Ahlback, Karin, et al. "The five trademarks of agile organizations." McKinsey, 22 January 2018, https://www.mckinsey.com/capabilities/people-and-organizational-performance/our-insights/the-five-trademarks-of-agile-organizations. Accessed 12 June 2024.

B Corporation. "B Impact Assessment Structure : Support Portal." Knowledge Base, 20 May 2020, https://kb.bimpactassessment.net/support/solutions/articles/43000574682-b-impact-assessment-structure. Accessed 12 June 2024.

Donegan, Patrick. "Who's vaulting into the C-suite? Trends changed fast in 2022." LinkedIn, 1 February 2023, https://www.linkedin.com/pulse/whos-vaulting-c-suite-trends-changed-fast-2022-george-anders/?trackingid=joiievmfqi6smbg%2bkwpciq%3d%3d. Accessed 13 June 2024.

Dyvik, Einar H. "Global companies 2021." Statista, 19 December 2023, https://www.statista.com/statistics/1260686/global-companies/. Accessed 13 June 2024.

"How the B Impact Assessment is Used." Knowledge Base, 20 May 2020, https://kb.bimpactassessment.net/support/solutions/articles/43000574679-how-the-b-impact-assessment-is-used. Accessed 12 June 2024.

Kiger, Patrick J., and Stefan J. Reichelstein. "Does It Pay to Link Executive

Compensation to ESG Goals?" Stanford Graduate School of Business, 13 July 2023, https://www.gsb.stanford.edu/insights/does-it-pay-link-executive-compensation-esg-goals. Accessed 13 June 2024.

Murray, Jane Kellogg. "Jobs in Diversity, Inclusion and Belonging Have Risen 123% Since May—Here's How To Get One." Indeed, 20 April 2023, https://www.indeed.com/career-advice/finding-a-job/diversity-inclusion-and-belonging-jobs-rise. Accessed 13 June 2024.

Percy, Sally. "How Servant Leaders Boost Profits And Employee Morale." Forbes, 15 July 2020, https://www.forbes.com/sites/sallypercy/2020/07/15/how-servant-leaders-boost-profits-and-employee-morale/. Accessed 13 June 2024.

Small Business & Entrepreneurship Council. "Small Business & Entrepreneurship Council." Small Business & Entrepreneurship Council, 2019, https://sbecouncil.org/about-us/facts-and-data/. Accessed 13 June 2024.

Sorace, Stephen. "Alaska Airlines plane had door panel blow out ahead of scheduled safety check: report." Fox Business, 13 March 2024, https://www.foxbusiness.com/lifestyle/alaska-airlines-plane-door-panel-blow-out-ahead-scheduled-safety-check-report. Accessed 13 June 2024.

Nerozzi, Timothy. "Boeing failed 33 out of 89 audits during FAA examination: report." Fox Business, 12 March 2024, Boeing failed 33 out of 89 audits during FAA examination: report. Accessed 12 July 2024.

"Tech Layoffs: US Companies With Job Cuts In and 2023 and 2024." Crunchbase News, 7 June 2024,

HTTPS://NEWS.CRUNCHBASE.COM/STARTUPS/TECH-LAYOFFS/. ACCESSED 13 JUNE 2024.

"UNPACKING THE 'B IMPACT SCORE' — WHAT IT IS AND WHY IT MATTERS." B LAB AUSTRALIA, 6 JULY 2022, HTTPS://BCORPORATION.COM.AU/BLOG/UNPACKING-THE-B-IMPACT-SCORE/. ACCESSED 12 JUNE 2024.

FORBES (2019) - "THE ROI OF LISTENING"

GALLUP (2018) - "THE RELATIONSHIP BETWEEN ENGAGEMENT AT WORK AND ORGANIZATIONAL OUTCOMES"

HARVARD BUSINESS REVIEW (2015) - "HOW GREAT MANAGERS INSPIRE THEIR EMPLOYEES"

GALLUP (2017) - "STATE OF THE AMERICAN WORKPLACE"

GREAT PLACE TO WORK INSTITUTE (2020) - "TRUST AND CULTURE"

BUSINESSOLVER (2021) - "STATE OF WORKPLACE EMPATHY STUDY"

MCLEOD, S. (2020). COGNITIVE BEHAVIORAL THERAPY (CBT). SIMPLY PSYCHOLOGY. RETRIEVED FROM HTTPS://WWW.SIMPLYPSYCHOLOGY.ORG/COGNITIVE-THERAPY.HTML

ALABI, K. O., & MAHMUDA, S. (2024). A REVIEW ON THE ASSESSMENT OF EFFECTIVE STRATEGIES FOR PROMOTING A DIVERSE AND INCLUSIVE WORKPLACE CULTURE: BIAS TRAINING AND EQUITABLE HIRING APPROACH. IJRESM, 7(5), 69-74. HTTPS://DOI.ORG/10.5281/ZENODO.11195260

BERNSTEIN, R., SALIPANTE, P., & WEISINGER, J. (2021). PERFORMANCE THROUGH DIVERSITY AND INCLUSION: LEVERAGING ORGANIZATIONAL PRACTICES FOR EQUITY

AND RESULTS. LONDON: ROUTLEDGE.
HTTPS://DOI.ORG/10.4324/9780367822484

BRCE, J. N., & KOGOVŠEK, D. (2020). INCLUSION, INCLUSIVE EDUCATION AND
INCLUSIVE COMMUNICATION. IN B. SAQIPI & S. BERČNIK (EDS.). SELECTED TOPICS IN
EDUCATION. ALBAS, TIRANË.

CHEN, C. (2023). REVIEW EXAMINING BIASES IN WORKPLACE HIRING AND PROMOTION
PROCESSES. CMC SENIOR THESES, 3221.
HTTPS://SCHOLARSHIP.CLAREMONT.EDU/CMC_THESES/3221

EDMONDSON, A. C., & BRANDBY, D. P. (2023). PSYCHOLOGICAL SAFETY COMES OF
AGE: OBSERVED THEMES IN AN ESTABLISHED LITERATURE. ANNUAL REVIEW OF
ORGANIZATIONAL PSYCHOLOGY AND ORGANIZATIONAL BEHAVIOR, 10(1), 55-78.
HTTPS://DOI.ORG/10.1146/ANNUREV-ORGPSYCH-120920-055217

ELKHWESKY, Z., SALEM, I. E., & BARAKAT, M. (2021). IMPORTANCE-
IMPLEMENTATION OF DISABILITY MANAGEMENT PRACTICES IN HOTELS: THE
MODERATING EFFECT OF TEAM ORIENTATION. JOURNAL OF MEDITERRANEAN TOURISM
RESEARCH, 1(1), 22-38. HTTPS://DOI.ORG/10.5038/2770-7555.1.11003

FRANCO, M. G. (2022). PLATONIC: HOW THE SCIENCE OF ATTACHMENT CAN HELP
YOU MAKE-AND KEEP-FRIENDS. NEW YORK, NY: G. P. PUTNAM'S SONS.

HARDY, J. H., TEY, K. S., CYRUS-LAI, W., MARTELL, R. F., OLSTAD, A., & UHLMANN,
E. L. (2022). BIAS IN CONTEXT: SMALL BIASES IN HIRING EVALUATIONS HAVE BIG
CONSEQUENCES. JOURNAL OF MANAGEMENT, 48(3), 657-692.
HTTPS://DOI.ORG/10.1177/0149206320982654

HUNT, D. V., LAYTON, D., & PRINCE, S. (2015, JANUARY 1). WHY DIVERSITY
MATTERS. MCKINSEY & COMPANY. RETRIEVED FROM

HTTPS://WWW.MCKINSEY.COM/CAPABILITIES/PEOPLE-AND-ORGANIZATIONAL-PERFORMANCE/OUR-INSIGHTS/WHY-DIVERSITY-MATTERS

LEVINE, S. R. (2020, JANUARY 15). DIVERSITY CONFIRMED TO BOOST INNOVATION AND FINANCIAL RESULTS. FORBES. RETRIEVED FROM HTTPS://WWW.FORBES.COM/SITES/FORBESINSIGHTS/2020/01/15/DIVERSITY-CONFIRMED-TO-BOOST-INNOVATION-AND-FINANCIAL-RESULTS/

PARKS, N., BARBIERI, F., SAIN, R., CAPELL, S., & KIRBY, B. (2024). THE BEHAVIOR OF SOCIAL JUSTICE: APPLYING BEHAVIOR ANALYSIS TO UNDERSTAND AND CHALLENGE INJUSTICE. ROUTLEDGE.

VENTURA, A., PARKS, N., CROWLEY, E., & URIARTE, D. (2020). FEEDBACK F!@#UPS AND HOW TO AVOID THEM: HOW TO USE THE PROVEN POWER OF BEHAVIOR SCIENCE TO IMPROVE PERFORMANCE FEEDBACK. MIAMI, FL: 305 PUBLISHING.

Made in the USA
Middletown, DE
19 September 2024